AFTER THE
GOLD RUSH

*Creating a True
Profession of
Software
Engineering*

Steve McConnell

Published by Microsoft Press
A Division of Microsoft Corporation
One Microsoft Way
Redmond, Washington 98052-6399

Library of Congress Cataloging-in-Publication Data pending.

Printed and bound in the United States of America.

1 2 3 4 5 6 7 8 9   QMQM   4 3 2 1 0 9

Distributed in Canada by Penguin Books Canada Limited.

A CIP catalogue record for this book is available from the British Library.

Microsoft Press books are available through booksellers and distributors worldwide.
For further information about international editions, contact your local Microsoft
Corporation office, or contact Microsoft Press International directly at fax (425) 936-
7329. Visit our Web site at mspress.microsoft.com.

Acquisitions Editor: Ben Ryan
Project Editor: Victoria Thulman

———◆———

"All rising to a great place is by a winding stair."

—*Francis Bacon*

———◆———

CONTENTS

Acknowledgments

I am grateful to the people who commented on significant sections of the book, including Jon Bentley, Steven Black, Robert C. Burns (The Boeing Company), Trevor Burridge, Augusto Coppola, Alan B. Corwin (Process Builder), Ryan Fleming, Pat Forman, Robert L. Glass (Computing Trends), David Goodman, Owain E Griffiths, Bradey Honsinger, Larry M. Hughes (Sprint), Robert E. Lee, Avonelle Lovhaug, Mike Lutz, Steve Mattingly, Grant McLaughlin, Brian P. McLean, Hank Meuret, Matt Peloquin, Steve Rinn, Kathy Rhode, Wm. Paul Rogers, Jay Silverman, André Sintzoff, Tim Starry, Steve Tockey, Leonard L. Tripp, Tom Ventser (DMR Consulting Group), Karl Wiegers, and Greg Wilson.

It was a pleasure to see the excellent book production team at Microsoft Press prepare this manuscript for publication in record time. Special thanks to Victoria Thulman, project editor. Thanks also to Microsoft Press staff Ben Ryan, Rob Nance, Cheryl Penner, and Paula Gorelick.

Finally, thanks to my wife, Tammy, for being a "book widow" one more time. She says she thinks that programmers should be "certified," but I'm not at all sure she means the same thing I do!

INTRODUCTION

———◆———

"It looks obvious until you try it."
—*IEEE Software*

———◆———

In the state of Texas, professional engineers were originally licensed in 1937 after a boiler explosion caused the deaths of more than 300 school children. At that time, the boiler part that failed was mechanical. Today that part's function is handled by software.[1] Good software has the potential to make our lives much better; bad software has the potential to make them much worse. The practices needed to create good software are well established and readily available, but there is a chasm between the average practice and the best. Consider these statistics:

◆ An aerospace company develops software for companies on a fixed-price basis. Their managers think they have problems: 3 percent of their projects overrun their budgets; 97 out of 100 are delivered on target. They don't know that the typical business systems project overruns its planned budget by about 100 percent and that only about a quarter are delivered within 25 percent of their original targets.

◆ A team developing software for the United States Air Force committed to a one-year schedule and a $2 million budget even though the most credible bid for the project was two years and $10 million. By using active risk management and sound fundamental development, the team delivered the project one month early. The software delighted its users and, one year later, only two defects had been found in operation. The project manager pointed out that the

---

1. Source citations and notes about related topics can be found in the "Notes" section at the end of the book.

project used techniques that had been known for years but were rarely used in practice. In contrast, the average software project does no risk management at all and overruns its schedule by more than 100 percent.

◆ An organization was determined to shorten its schedules, and focused on systematic process improvement. It attained an average of 23 percent schedule reduction per year for six years, for a total reduction of 91 percent. Most organizations have no process improvement program in place. In the worst organizations, productivity has been seen to erode from one year to the next.

◆ An organization that committed to achieving outstanding quality attained an average of 39 percent reduction in its post-release defect rate every year for a period of nine years—a cumulative reduction of 99 percent. The average organization doesn't even know what its post-release defect rate is.

The view from the top looks good, but the view from the vantage point of the average project leaves much to be desired, as the victims of many well-known software disasters will attest: Problems with the baggage handling system caused a delay of more than a year in opening Denver International Airport. Estimates of the delay's cost ranged as high as $1.1 million per day. The FAA's Advanced Automation System overran its planned budget by about $3 billion. The IRS bumbled an $8-billion software modernization program that cost U.S. taxpayers $50 billion per year in lost revenue. After topping $44 million, a long series of overruns forced the state of California to cancel its motor vehicle registration system. The B-2 bomber wouldn't fly on its maiden flight because of a software problem. The Ariane 5 rocket blew up on its maiden launch because of a software error. In Seattle, computer-controlled ferries caused more than a dozen dock crashes in the 1980s, resulting in damage worth more than $7 million. The state of Washington recommended spending more than $3 million to revert the operation of ferries to manual controls.

Even software that isn't considered mission-critical is being used in important applications. The project lead of Lotus Symphony received a call from a surgeon who was using Symphony to analyze patient data during open heart surgery. *Newsweek* magazine printed pictures of the Nicaraguan contras planning operations using Excel on portable PCs. The Microsoft Excel technical support team received calls from the battlefield during Operation Desert Storm.

In the rush to get the current project out the door, software developers sometimes lose sight of the big-picture reasons their software development jobs matter. Whether we like it or not, software is important. It affects people's lives. And the development practices most commonly used to produce software are not up to the task. As Fred Brooks pointed out more than 10 years ago, "The gap between the best software engineering practice and the average practice is very wide—perhaps wider than in any other engineering discipline."

It's time for software development to grow up.

The Purpose of This Book

This book is about creating a true profession of software engineering. Significant developments are under way that will affect the careers of practicing programmers, including initiatives in education, professional development, certification, and licensing. Some of these developments are well thought out and positive; others are being forced and need to be improved before they're standardized. Software development is changing, whether programmers recognize it or not. Programmers who aren't paying attention could easily find themselves working as twenty-first century software janitors. This book describes the occupation of computer programming as it exists today and the profession of software engineering as it can exist in the future.

Who Should Read This Book

If you develop software for a living, important developments are under way that will affect your career and your ability to call yourself a "software engineer." They apply to you whether you are a programmer, tester, requirements analyst, manager, or other software worker.

If you manage a software organization, you should know about the incredible potential of systematic approaches to software development—in other words, software engineering.

If you are an educator, you should understand industry's needs for professional software development—what is useful and what is not—and the elements of a complete software engineering curriculum.

If you are a student who wants to work in the software field, you will need to know about the body of knowledge that makes up the field of software engineering and what a career in software engineering will look like.

If you are a public policy maker, you should know how software development got to be the way it is now so that you can make sensible policy decisions related to licensing and regulating software, software developers, and companies that create software.

Key Questions

This book is organized as a set of essays. They can be read individually or together, and they are all related to the theme of creating a true profession of software engineering. They address the following questions:

- What is software engineering?

- Why isn't regular computer programming good enough?

- Why do we need a profession of software engineering?

- Why is *engineering* the best model for a software development profession?

- Will software engineers have to be licensed? Will *you* have to be licensed?

- What does a software engineer have to know?

- What can you do while the software field is getting its act together?

This book focuses on software engineering in the United States and Canada. Many of the issues involved in establishing a profession are legal and cultural, and they vary among countries. To keep the narrative straightforward, I have deliberately maintained a North American focus.

Prospecting for Software Engineering

Most software development practices in common use today are seriously outdated and ineffective. This situation arises from lack of initial education, lack of continuing professional development, lack of time for personal improvement, lack of professional standards, treatment of software as a craft rather than as an engineering discipline, and many other reasons.

Practices exist today that make software engineering possible. The best companies are already using them, and these practices provide the companies with formidable advantages. Industry researchers have long observed

10-to-1 differences in productivity between different organizations competing in the same industries. More recently, researchers have observed differences as large as 600 to 1. The most effective organizations are doing very well indeed.

The benefits of creating a true profession of software engineering are so compelling that, I believe, 25 years from now organizations that today resist the movement toward software engineering will be viewed the same way as farmers who resisted crop rotation or businesses that resisted the telephone.

Practitioners who protest that software engineering is not possible are generally misinformed or simply afraid to change. But the fact that software engineering is possible does not mean that it is easy. For software engineering to achieve the status of a true profession, many organizations will have to work together, including the engineering community, the software community, the academic community, accreditation agencies, and state legislatures.

"If it ain't broke, don't fix it," the saying goes. Common software development practices are seriously broken, and the cost of not fixing them has become extreme. Traditional thinking would have it that change presents the greatest risk. In software's case, the greatest risk lies with not changing—staying mired in unhealthy, profligate development practices instead of switching to practices that were proven more effective many years ago.

How to change? That is the central topic of the rest of the book.

THE TAR PIT

1

Software Dinosaurs

---◆---

*"He that will not apply new remedies must expect new
evils for time is the greatest innovator."*
—Francis Bacon

---◆---

In 1975, Fred Brooks compared the development of large software systems to dinosaurs, woolly mammoths, and saber-toothed tigers fighting the glutinous grip of the tar pit.[1] Brooks predicted that the software engineering tar pit would continue to be sticky for a long time to come. The

---

1. Citations for data and further reading can be found in the "Notes" section at the end of the book.

problems that Brooks described twenty-five years ago were not new when he described them, and the software community has now had another quarter century to work on them. How much has the situation changed?

Schedule pressure is a common feature of today's projects. According to some estimates, excessive schedule pressure occurs in about 75 percent of all medium-size projects and in 90 percent or more of all large projects. Overtime is more the norm than the exception. Internet startups are known for the long hours they expect from their employees, and stories of programmers sleeping under their desks abound. But this isn't a new phenomenon. As far back as the mid-1960s, one report stated that, "In many companies, programmers faced with deadlines have been known to spend nights in their offices." In 1975, Fred Brooks pointed out that "more software projects have gone awry for lack of calendar time than all other causes combined." Schedule overruns have been around for at least 30 years (probably since time immemorial).

Many people today complain about the shortage of qualified software developers. Experts estimate that North America is now experiencing a software personnel shortage of about 10 percent. This is not a new problem either. Thirty years ago, total employment was estimated at 100,000 programming jobs in the United States, and experts estimated that 50,000 additional jobs were available—a 33 percent labor shortage that makes today's 10 percent labor shortage seem almost insignificant.

The scope of today's large software projects seems daunting, and a natural tendency is to think that no one ever attempted projects of the scope we now face. Yet even a huge project such as the initial development of Microsoft Windows NT has historical precedents. The initial Windows NT project required about 1,500 staff-years of effort, but the development of IBM's OS/360, which was completed in 1966, required more than three times as much effort.

Recent surveys have found that the most frequent causes of software project failure have to do with requirements problems—requirements that are too vague to be implemented, that contradict each other, or that change frequently and wreak havoc on the system design. But requirements problems are not new. Back in 1969, Robert Frosch observed that a system could "satisfy the letter of the specification and still not be very satisfactory."

Modern developers rack their brains trying to keep up with the frenetic pace of change brought on by Internet development. How do you keep up with new languages, shifting standards, and vendors that release new products every few months? To those of us who were in the software world 15 years ago, this predicament sounds an awful lot like the mid-1980s when the IBM PC began to revolutionize corporate computing.

When the Fortran programming language was developed in 1954–58, it was supposed to eliminate the need for computer programming—scientists and engineers could simply enter their formulas into the computer, and the computer would translate the formulas for them, thus the name FORmula TRANslation. Of course, Fortran didn't eliminate programming; it just reduced the need for machine-language programming. From time to time we still hear about the promise of automatic programming—computers will become so advanced that the need for computer programmers will disappear. But this conjecture was already a well-polished chestnut 30 years ago when Gene Bylinsky reported that, "Predictions of businessmen blithely conversing with their omnipotent machines in plain English still get played up regularly in the press." The reality is that defining problems in painstaking detail is difficult work that can't be automated. That aspect of computer programming will not go away. New tools are useful, but not a substitute for clear thinking. I made that point in my 1996 book *Rapid Development*; Robert Frosch had already made the same point in *IEEE Spectrum* 30 years earlier.

Internet developers talk about development in Internet time. The Internet makes it possible for developers to roll out revisions to their programs with unprecedented ease. CDs and DVDs don't have to be duplicated; users can download upgrades electronically, making delivery of upgrades quick and inexpensive. This ease of distribution contributes to pressure to release upgrades frequently in response to user requests. Internet developers say that users would rather get the software quickly than have it be perfect. Users will tolerate low reliability. According to Internet developers, "It's better to be first than right."

How unprecedented are these dynamics really? Some Internet developers think they are unique to web projects, but industry old-timers know better: low rollout cost, easy corrections, and low cost of failure sound like a good old-fashioned in-house mainframe production environment.

The common threads tying together over 25 years of software development—schedule pressure, staff shortages, large projects, faulty requirements, volatile technology, and even development in Internet time—are a source of both comfort and despair. The despair arises from the fact that some problems have been with us for a quarter century or more and are still common. We truly have been stuck in the tar pit a long time. But we've been staring at the same problems long enough to recognize some patterns, and some software organizations have escaped the tar pit's sticky grip. Therein lies the comfort.

Fool's Gold

---◆---

"Hope is a good breakfast, but it is a bad supper."
—*Francis Bacon*

---◆---

Software problems have persisted partly because of the allure of a few common, ineffective practices. During the California gold rush in the late 1840s and early 1850s, some prospectors were deceived by fool's gold— iron pyrite—a substance that has the luster and sparkle of gold. Unlike gold, iron pyrite is flaky, brittle, and virtually valueless. Experienced miners know that real gold is soft and malleable, and doesn't break under pressure. For 50 years, software developers have been succumbing to the temptation of their own fool's gold. They are drawn to flawed practices that have a seductive appeal, but like iron pyrite, the practices that make up software's fool's gold are flaky, brittle, and virtually valueless.

Moving the Block

Look back many centuries before the California gold rush, and suppose that you are working on one of the ancient pyramids. You are given the assignment to move an enormous stone block 10,000 meters from a river to the site of a pyramid under construction, as shown in Figure 2-1. You are given 100 days to move the block and 20 people with which to move it.

FIGURE 2-1   *One way to think of a software project is as a heavy block of stone. You must either move the block one day closer to the final destination each day, or you must do something that will enable you to traverse the remaining distance in one less day.*

You are allowed to use any method you like to move the block to its destination. Each day, you have to move the block an average of 100 meters closer to the pyramid, or you have to do something that will reduce the number of days needed to travel the remaining distance.

Some block-moving teams might immediately begin pushing the block, trying to move it with brute force. With a very small block, this method might work, but with a heavy block resting directly on desert sand, this approach won't move the block very quickly, if at all. If a team moves the block 10 meters per day, the fact that the block is moving at all might be satisfying, but the team is actually falling 90 meters per day behind. "Progress" doesn't necessarily mean *sufficient* progress.

The smart block-moving team wouldn't jump straight into trying to move the block with brute force. They know that for all but the smallest blocks, they will need to spend time planning how to move the block before they put their muscles into it. After analyzing their assignment, they might decide to cut down a few trees and use the tree trunks as rollers, as shown in Figure 2-2. That plan will take a day or two, but chances are pretty good that it will increase the speed at which they can move the block.

What if trees aren't readily available, and the team has to spend several days hiking up river to find some? The hike is still probably a good investment, especially since the team that begins by trying to use brute force will move the block only a fraction of the distance needed each day.

The smart block-moving team might also want to prepare the surface over which they will be moving the block. Instead of pushing it across the sand, they might want to create a level roadway first, which would be an especially good idea if they had more to move than this one block.

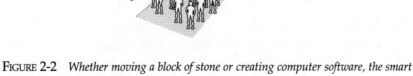

FIGURE 2-2   *Whether moving a block of stone or creating computer software, the smart team takes time at the beginning of the project to plan its work so that it can proceed quickly and efficiently.*

A really sophisticated block-moving team might start with the roller and road system, and eventually realize that having only the minimum number of rollers available forces them to stop work too often; they have to move the back roller to the front of the block every time they move the block forward one roller-width. By having a few extra rollers on hand and assigning some people to move the rollers from back to front, the team is better able to maintain its momentum.

The team might also realize that pushing the block is limited by how many people can fit around the block's base. They create a harness so that they can pull the block from the front at the same time they're pushing it from behind, as illustrated in Figure 2-3. As the work is divided among more people, each person's work becomes easier, and the faster pace is actually more sustainable than the slower one.

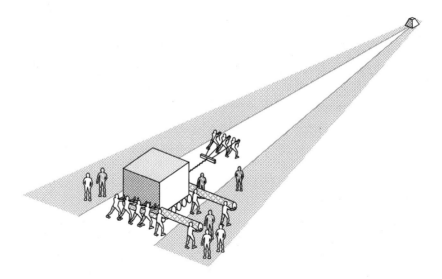

FIGURE 2-3   *Smart teams continuously look for ways to work more efficiently.*

Stone Blocks and Software

How does this block moving relate to software? The movement of the stone block is analogous to creating source code. If you have 100 days to complete a software project, you either need to complete one hundredth of the source code each day, or you need to do work that will allow you to complete the remaining source code faster. The work of creating source code is much less tangible than the work of moving a stone block, and progress at the beginning of a software project can be harder to gauge. Software projects are vulnerable to a "last-minute syndrome" in which the project team has little sense of urgency at the beginning of a project, fritters away days on end, and works itself into a desperate frenzy by the end of the project. Thinking of a project's source code as a stone block makes clear that you can't hope to conduct a successful project by sprinting at the end. Every day, a software project manager should ask, "Did we move the block one day closer to our destination today? If not, did we reduce our remaining work by one day?"

Another way that moving a stone block relates to software is that no matter how much planning you do, at some point you have to move the block; you have to write the source code. Creating source code on all but the smallest projects involves an enormous amount of detail work, and you can easily underestimate how much.

Code-and-Fix Development

Overpreparation's opposite—not focusing enough on making rollers and preparing roadways—is by far the more common problem in software. About 75 percent of software project teams begin their projects by hurling themselves against the block and trying to move it with brute force. This approach, called "code-and-fix development," is defined as jumping straight into coding without planning or designing the software first. Sometimes teams use this approach because their software developers are anxious to begin coding. Sometimes they follow it because managers or customers are eager to see tangible signs of progress.

The problem with the code-and-fix approach, as with the brute-force approach to moving the stone block, is that quick movement off the starting line doesn't necessarily translate into quick movement toward the finish line. The team that uses a more advanced approach is putting a framework in place that will allow the project to spin up to a high level of productivity and finish efficiently. Essentially, the team is putting rollers under the block, clearing the roadway, and preparing to focus the energy of the project team. In contrast, the code-and-fix project gets off to an early start but can't sustain the brute force approach. Typically, such an approach leads to the creation of hundreds or thousands of defects early in the project. Several studies have found that 40–80 percent of a typical software project's budget goes into fixing defects that were created earlier on the same project.

Figure 2-4 illustrates the way that productivity erodes over time on a code-and-fix project. Little or no effort is invested in planning and process management at the beginning of the project. Some small amount of effort goes into thrashing (unproductive work), but most work goes into coding. As the project moves forward, fixing defects becomes an increasingly prominent feature of the project. By the end of the project, the team is spending most of its time fixing the defects that it created earlier.

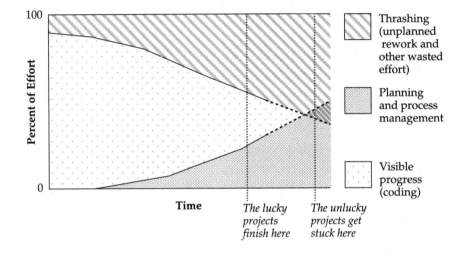

FIGURE 2-4 *Using a code-and-fix approach, the lucky projects finish while they are still eking out a small amount of productive work. The unlucky projects get stuck in a zone where 100 percent of their effort is consumed by thrashing, planning, and process management. (Source: adapted from McConnell,* Software Project Survival Guide, *1988.)*

As Figure 2-4 suggests, the lucky code-and-fix projects are brought to completion while they are still scraping out some small amount of coding progress. The unlucky projects get stuck on the far right side of the diagram where 100 percent of their available effort is consumed by planning, process management, and thrashing, and they are not making any coding progress.

This gloomy picture is no exaggeration. Several studies have reported that about 25 percent of all software projects are eventually canceled. At the time the average project is canceled, it is 100 percent over budget and caught in an extended debug, test, and fix cycle—thrashing. The reason the project is canceled is the perception that its quality problems are insurmountable.

The irony of this pattern is that unsuccessful projects eventually do as much planning and process management as the successful project. The unsuccessful projects still have to implement defect tracking to manage all the bugs being reported. They begin estimating more carefully as the release date approaches. As pressure to release increases, they may re-estimate as often as every week or, in some cases, as often as every day. They spend time managing expectations of project stakeholders, convincing them that the project will eventually be released. They may begin imposing standards for debugging new code before it is integrated with already-debugged code. Because these practices are begun late in the project, however, the benefits are leveraged over only a small part of the project. The practices implemented on the unsuccessful project are different from the practices a more effective organization would implement in the early stages of a project—in fact, many of the practices implemented late in the unsuccessful project wouldn't even be needed if the project had been run well from the beginning.

As Figure 2-5 illustrates, the most sophisticated organizations—those that produce the most reliable software for the least cost and with shortest schedules—spend a relatively small percentage of their budgets on the coding part of a project. The least sophisticated organizations spend practically their whole budgets on coding and fixing bugs in their code. Their total budgets are much higher because they don't lay any groundwork for working efficiently. (I'll return to this in more detail in Chapter 7.)

Code-and-fix development continues to be used because it is appealing in two ways. First, it allows the project team to show signs of progress immediately—they can begin moving the stone block 10 meters per day the first day while the more effective team is still out cutting down trees, preparing the roadway for a smooth trip, and showing no visible signs of actually moving the block. If managers and customers aren't very sophisticated about the dynamics of a successful project—and most are not—a code-and-fix approach looks appealing because the project gets off to a quick start. The second reason code-and-fix development is appealing is that it requires no training. In the software industry, the average level of training in software engineering is low, and so by default code-and-fix development is the most common approach. It seems attractive at first glance, but it is a form of software fool's gold, and experienced software developers recognize it as having little value.

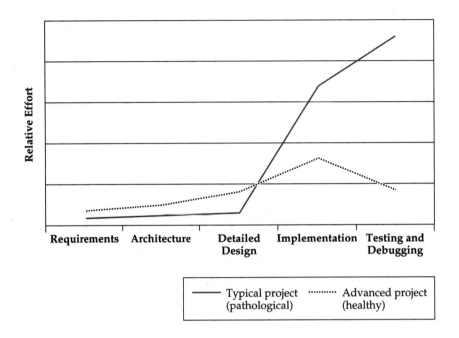

FIGURE 2-5 *Advanced software development approaches require more work during the early stages of the project to eliminate an enormous amount of unnecessary work in the later stages of a project.*

Resisting Code-and-Fix Development

The sparkle and luster of quick, early progress is one reason that customers and managers continue to fall for code-and-fix development. When project stakeholders want to influence the methods used on a project, they typically do it at the beginning of the project. As Figure 2-6 shows, the code-and-fix approach demonstrates rapid headway at the beginning of the project, but the advanced approach doesn't produce much visible progress.

The advanced project team can't demonstrate that it is making faster progress than a code-and-fix project team when the customer or manager is looking for executable code at the beginning of a project. So the best time to convince project stakeholders to use advanced software development practices is at the end of a code-and-fix project, when the dynamics illustrated in Figure 2-6 are painfully obvious to everyone involved.

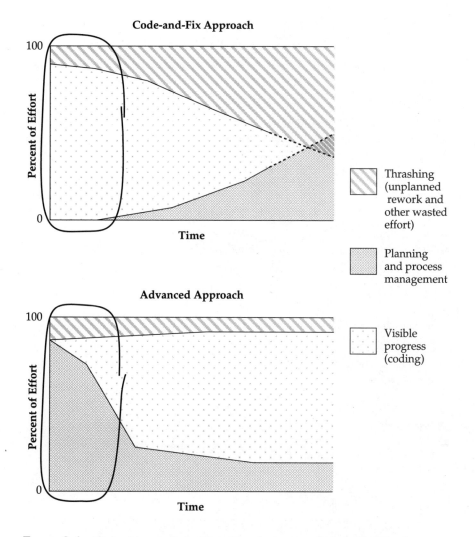

FIGURE 2-6   *It's hard to convince customers and managers that advanced development approaches are better if they insist on seeing source code early in the project.*

Focus on Quality

You might assume that a software project's schedule can be shortened when developers spend less time on testing or technical reviews. "Needless overhead!" say people with a taste for code-and-fix development. Industry experience indicates otherwise. An attempt to trade quality for cost or schedule actually results in increased cost and a longer schedule.

As Figure 2-7 illustrates, projects that remove about 95 percent of their defects prior to release are the most productive; they spend the least time fixing their own defects. Beyond about 95 percent defect removal, projects have to expend extra effort to improve quality. Projects falling short of 95 percent defect removal can become more efficient by removing more defects sooner. Approximately 75 percent of software projects remove less than 95 percent of their defects. For these projects, the attempt to trade quality for cost or schedule is another example of fool's gold. It's also an example of a software project dynamic that isn't really new. IBM discovered 20 years ago that projects that focused their efforts on attaining the shortest schedules had high frequencies of cost and schedule overruns. Projects that focused on achieving low defect counts had the best schedules and the highest productivities.

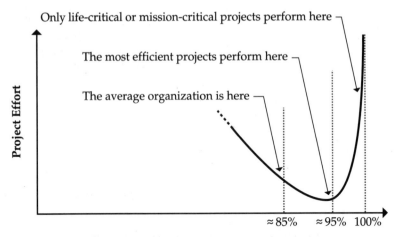

Percentage of Defects Removed Before Release

FIGURE 2-7 *Up to a point, the projects that achieve the lowest defect rates also achieve the shortest schedules. Most projects can shorten their schedules by focusing on fixing defects earlier. (Source: adapted from Jones,* Applied Software Measurement: Assuring Productivity and Quality, *2d ed., 1977.)*

Some Fool's Gold Is Silver

Technologies and methodologies that are associated with extravagant productivity claims are called "silver bullets" because they are supposed to slay
the werewolf of low productivity. For decades, the software industry has
been plagued by claims that the UmptyFratz Innovation dramatically improves development speed. In the 1960s, on-line programming was associated with this claim. In the 1970s, third-generation languages were. In the
1980s, advocates for artificial intelligence and CASE tools made this promise. In the 1990s, object-oriented programming was lauded as the next great
productivity boon.

Suppose that a stone-block project team starts out using the brute-force
method to move the stone block. After a few days, the team leader sees that
progress isn't fast enough to meet the project's goals. Fortunately, he has
heard of an amazing animal called an "elephant." An elephant can weigh
almost 200 times as much as an adult human being and is extremely powerful. The project leader mounts an expedition to capture and bring back an
elephant to help the team move the block. After a three-week safari, the team
returns with a captive elephant. They harness the magnificent beast to the
block and crack the whip. They hold their collective breath, waiting to see
just how fast the elephant will move the block. They may even finish ahead
of schedule! As they watch, the elephant begins pulling the block forward
much faster than the team of humans had ever been able to accomplish. But
then, unexpectedly, the elephant rears on its hind legs. It breaks its harness,
tramples two of its handlers, and runs off at 25 miles per hour, never to be
seen again (as shown in Figure 2-8). The stone-block team is dejected: "Maybe
we should have spent more time learning how to handle the elephant before we started using him on a real project." They wasted more than 20 percent of their schedule looking for the elephant, lost two teammates, and are
no closer to the goal than when they started. That, in a nutshell, is silver
bullet syndrome.

FIGURE 2-8   *Silver bullet innovations often fall short of expectations.*

The elephant analogy is more apt than you might think. Robert L. Glass chronicles 16 troubled projects in *Software Runaways*. Four of the projects he describes expected to be breakthrough successes because of their use of silver bullet innovations. Instead, they ended up failing because of the same innovations.

A special kind of silver bullet is forged from attempts to implement organizational process improvement half-heartedly. Some organizations try to implement organizational improvement with buzzwords—TQM, QFD, SW-CMM, Zero Defects, Six Sigma, Continuous Improvement, Statistical Process Control. These are all valuable practices when properly applied— that is, when focusing on the substance of the practice and not just the form. But each of these practices is virtually worthless when applied only as a buzzword. Some organizations cycle through the buzzwords in 12-month intervals, as if ritualistically chanting the initials of a current management fad could call forth improvements in quality and productivity. A special place in low-productivity hell is reserved for these organizations. After years of Management By Buzzword (MBB), entire staffs become cynical about organizational improvement initiatives in general, which makes escaping code-and-fix development even harder than usual.

The right innovation applied to the right project, supported by appropriate training, and deployed with realistic expectations can be tremendously beneficial when implemented as a long-term strategy. But new innovations aren't magic, and they aren't easy. Silver bullets are fool's gold because they are often embraced with a get-rich-quick attitude. They are adopted to achieve short-term gains, without appropriate training, and with no management of the risks involved. Like iron pyrite, experienced managers and software developers should know better than to be fooled by them.

Software Isn't Soft

One more kind of fool's gold is the belief that software is soft. Hardware is "hard" because it is difficult to change. Software was originally called "soft" because it was easy to change, and very small programs at the dawn of computer programming probably were easy to change. As software systems have become more complex, however, this notion that software is easy to change has become one of the most pernicious ideas in software development.

Several studies have found that requirements changes—attempts to take advantage of software's supposed softness—are among the most common sources of cost and schedule overruns. They are also a major factor in project cancellations; in some cases, requirements changes can destabilize a product to such a degree that it can't be finished at all.

A simple example illustrates why software isn't as soft as people think. Suppose that you are asked to design a system that will initially print a set of five reports and eventually print a set of ten reports. You have several kinds of flexibility—softness—that you will need to be concerned about:

- Is ten an upper limit on the number of reports?
- Will future reports be similar to the initial five reports?
- Will all of the reports always be printed?
- Will the reports always be printed in the same order?
- To what extent will users be able to customize the reports?
- Will users be allowed to define their own reports?
- Will the reports be translated into other languages?

No matter how carefully the software is designed, there will always be a point at which the software is no longer "soft." In the case of the reports, as the software is modified, any of the following areas could turn out to be "hard":

- Defining more than ten reports
- Defining a new report that is different from the initial set of reports
- Printing a subset of the reports
- Printing the reports in a user-defined order
- Allowing users to customize reports
- Allowing users to define an entire custom report
- Translating the reports into another language that uses a Latin alphabet
- Translating the reports into another language that uses a non-Latin alphabet or is read right to left

What's interesting about this example is that I can ask a whole hat full of questions about the "softness" of the reports without knowing anything whatsoever about the specific reports or about the system that will print the reports. Simply knowing that there are "some reports" raises many general questions about the different degrees of softness.

Saying that software developers should always design software to be as flexible as possible is tempting, but flexibility is an almost infinitely variable entity, and it comes at a price. If the user really wants a standard set of five preformatted reports, always printed as a set, and always printed in the same order in the same language, the software developer should not create an elaborate utility that allows the user to generate highly customized reports. That utility could easily cost the customer 100–1000 times as much as providing the basic functionality the user really needs. The user (or client or manager) has a responsibility to help software developers define exactly how much flexibility is needed.

Flexibility costs money up front. Limiting flexibility saves money up front, but typically costs disproportionately more money later. The difficult engineering judgment is weighing the known present need against the possible future need and determining how "soft" or "hard" to make the "ware."

How Fool's Gold Pans Out

In conclusion, we hold the following software truths to be self-evident (after careful examination, anyway):

- The success of a software project depends on not writing source code too early in the project. *BuT PLANNING AND DESIGNING INSTEAD*

- You can't reduce cost or shorten a schedule by allowing more defects unless you're working on life-critical systems. For most kinds of software, focus on reducing defects; cost and schedule will follow.

- Silver bullets are hazardous to a project's health, though software industry history suggests that vendors will continue to claim otherwise.

- Half-hearted process improvement is an especially damaging kind of silver bullet because it undermines future improvement attempts.

- Despite its name, software isn't soft unless it's made that way in the first place, and doing so is expensive.

The software world has had 50 years to learn these self-evident truths. As I will show in later chapters, the most successful people and organizations have taken them to heart. In the unsuccessful organizations, people continue to mistake iron pyrite for the real thing. Learning to resist fool's gold—and resist it consistently—is one of the first steps the software industry must take on the road to establishing a true profession of software engineering.

3

Orphans Preferred

———◆———

*"Wanted: Young, skinny, wirey fellows not over 18.
Must be expert riders willing to risk death daily.
Orphans preferred. Wages $25 per week."*
—Pony Express advertisement, 1860

———◆———

*"We realize the skills, intellect and personality we seek are
rare, and our compensation plan reflects that. In return, we
expect* TOTAL AND ABSOLUTE COMMITMENT *to project success—
overcoming all obstacles to create applications on time
and within budget."*
—Software developer advertisement, 1995

———◆———

The stereotypical programmer is a shy young man who works in a
darkened room, intensely concentrating on magical incantations that
coax the computer to do his bidding. He can concentrate 12–16 hours at
a time, often working through the night to realize his artistic vision. He

subsists on pizza and Twinkies. When interrupted, the programming creature responds violently, hurling strings of cryptic acronyms at his interrupter— "TCP/IP, RPC, RCS, SCSI, ISA, ACM, and IEEE!" The programmer breaks his intense concentration only to attend Star Trek conventions and watch Monty Python reruns. He is sometimes regarded as an indispensable genius, sometimes as an eccentric artist. Vital information is stored in his head and his head alone. He is secure knowing that, valuable as he is, precious few people compete for his job.

USA Today reported that the techie nerd stereotype is so well entrenched that students in every grade ranked computer jobs near the bottom of their lists of career choices. The *Wall Street Journal* reported that film crews have difficulty presenting stories about leading-edge software companies in an interesting way because every story starts with "an office park, a cubicle, and a guy sitting there with a box on his desk." Sometimes the stereotype is fostered even inside the profession. The associate director of Stanford University's computer science program was quoted by the *New York Times* as saying that software jobs are "mind-numbingly boring."

How much of the stereotype is true, and what effect does it have on the programming occupation? To find out, let's look first at the programmer's personality then at the other elements of the stereotype.

The Meyers-Briggs Type Indicator

A common means of categorizing personality was developed by Katherine Briggs and Isabel Briggs Meyers and is called the Meyers-Briggs Type Indicator, or MBTI. The MBTI categorizes personality types in four ways:

◆ *Extroversion (E) or Introversion (I)*   Extroverts are oriented toward the outside world of people and things. Introverts are more interested in the inner world of ideas.

◆ *Sensing (S) or Intuition (N)*   This category refers to how a person prefers to receive decision-making data. The sensing person focuses on known facts, concrete data, and experience. The intuitive person looks for possibilities and focuses on concepts and theories.

◆ *Thinking (T) or Feeling (F)*   This category refers to a person's decision-making style. The thinker makes decisions based on objective analysis and logic; the feeler relies on subjective feelings and emotions.

◆   *Perceiving (P) or Judging (J)*   The perceiving person prefers flexibility and open-ended possibility, whereas the judging person prefers order and control.

After a person takes the MBTI test, that person is assigned one letter from each of the four categories, resulting in a designation such as *ISTJ* or *ENTJ*. These letters indicate an individual's personality tendencies or preferences; they don't necessarily indicate how a person will react in specific circumstances. For example, some people might have a natural preference for *I* (introversion) but have developed their *E* (extroversion) so that they can be more effective in a business setting. Test results might indicate such people are introverts even though most business associates would classify them as extroverts.

MBTI Results for Software Developers

Two large studies have found that the most common personality type for software developers is *ISTJ* (introversion, sensing, thinking, judging), a type that tends to be serious and quiet, practical, orderly, logical, and successful through concentration and thoroughness. *ISTJ*s comprise 25–40 percent of software developers.

Programmers are indeed introverts. One-half to two-thirds of the software development population is introverted compared to about one-quarter of the general population. One reason the majority of software developers are *I*s might be that more *I*s pursue higher education and programmers are more educated than average. About 60 percent of software developers have attained at least a bachelor's degree, compared to about 25 percent of the general population.

The *S/N* (sensing/intuition) and *T/F* (thinking/feeling) attributes are particularly interesting because they describe an individual's decision-making style. Eighty to ninety percent of software developers are *T*s, compared to about 50 percent of the general population. Compared to the average, *T*s are more logical, analytical, scientific, dispassionate, cold, impersonal, concerned with matters of truth, and unconcerned with people's feelings.

Programmers are approximately evenly split between *S*s and *N*s, and the difference between the two will be immediately recognizable to most software developers. *S*s are methodical, live in the world of what can be accomplished now; are precise, concrete, and practical; like to specialize; and like to develop a single idea in depth rather than several ideas at once. *N*s are inventive, live in the world of possibility and theories, like to generalize, and like to explore many alternative ideas. An example of an *S* is an expert programmer who is intimately acquainted with every detail of a specific programming language or technology. An example of an *N* is a designer who considers wide-ranging possibilities and shrugs off low-level technical issues as "implementation details." *S*s sometimes aggravate *N*s because *S*s go deep into technical details before *N*s feel the breadth has been adequately explored. *N*s sometimes aggravate *S*s because *N*s jump from one design idea to the next before *S*s feel they have explored any particular technical area in sufficient depth.

Personality Characteristics of Great Designers

MBTI provides some insight into typical programmer personalities, but it isn't the final word. Many programmers aspire to be great designers. What are the personality characteristics of great designers? One study of designers in general (not just software developers) found that the most creative problem solvers seem to move easily between the *S/N*, *T/F*, and *P/J* distinctions. These individuals move back and forth between the holistic and sequential, the intuitive and logical, and the theoretical and specific; and they are able to look at problems from many different points of view. Leonardo da Vinci and Albert Einstein are examples of such great designers (although I don't believe they ever took the MBTI).

Great designers have a large set of standard patterns that they apply to each new problem. If the problem fits an existing pattern, the great designer can easily solve it using a familiar technique.

Great designers have mastery of the tools they use.

Great designers aren't afraid of complexity, and some of the best are drawn to it. But their goal is to make the seemingly complex simple. As Einstein said, everything should be made as simple as possible, but no simpler. The French writer and aircraft designer Antoine de Saint-Exupéry made much the same point when he said, "You know you have achieved perfection in design not when you have nothing more to add, but when you have nothing more to take away."

Great designers seek out criticism of their work. The feedback loop that criticism supports allows them to try out and discard many possible solutions.

Great designers usually have experience on failed projects and have made a point of learning from their failures. They experiment with alternatives. Their creativity often leads them to dead ends, but they discover and correct their mistakes quickly. They have the tenacity to continue trying options even after other designers have given up.

Great designers are not afraid of using brute force to solve a problem. Thomas Edison worked on the problem of designing a filament for an electric light bulb for nearly two years. An assistant once asked him how he could keep trying after failing so many times. Edison didn't understand the question. In his mind, he hadn't failed at all. He is supposed to have replied, "What failure? I know thousands of things that do not work."

Great designers must be creative to generate numerous candidate design solutions. A great deal of research on creativity has revealed some common themes. Creative people are curious, and their curiosity covers a wide range of interests. They have high energy. They are self-confident and independent enough to explore ideas that other people think are foolish. They value their own judgment. They are intellectually honest, which helps them differentiate what they really think from what the conventional wisdom says they should think.

Great designers have a restless desire to *create*—to make things. That desire might be to create a building, an electronic circuit, or a computer program. They have a bias toward action. Great designers aren't satisfied merely to learn facts; they feel compelled to *apply* what they have learned to real-world situations. To the great designer, not applying knowledge is tantamount to not having obtained the knowledge in the first place.

Programmers live for the "aha" insights that produce breakthrough design solutions. I think this is one reason that software developers' affinity for Monty Python makes more sense than it might at first appear. Monty Python flouts social conventions using extremely unorthodox juxtapositions of elements of time and culture. The same independent, out-of-the-box thinking that gives rise to Monty Python's scripts can also give rise to the innovative technical design solutions that programmers strive for.

People outside software development might think of computer programming as dry and uncreative. People inside software development know that some of the most exciting projects of our times could not be accomplished without the contributions of highly creative individuals. Movie animation, the space program, computer games, medical technology—it's hard to find a leading-edge area that doesn't depend on the software developer's creativity. Software developers know that computer programming gives them a medium in which they can create something out of nothing, an experience that provides them with the same satisfaction that some individuals obtain from sculpting, painting, or writing. "Mind numbingly boring?" I don't think so.

Total and Absolute Commitment

The stereotype of the programmer working 12–16 hours at a time contains more than a grain of truth, however, and the Pony Express ad at the beginning of this chapter could almost describe some of today's software developers. To be an effective developer, you must be able to concentrate exclusively on the programming task. Such concentration exacts a penalty. While concentrating on a programming project, you lose track of time. One morning you look up, and it's 2:00 P.M.—you missed lunch. One Friday evening you look up, and it's 11:00 P.M.—you stood up your date or neglected to tell your spouse you were coming home late. One October you look up and realize that the summer is over and you missed it again because you spent the past three months concentrating on an interesting project. Work can exclude family, friends, and other social ties. Here is Pascal Zachary's description of programmer commitment on the Microsoft Windows NT project:

> Work pervades their existence. Friends fade into the background. The ties of marriage fray or rip apart. Children are neglected or deferred. Hobbies wither. Computer code comes to mean everything. If private dreams are nursed at all, it is only to ease the pain of creating NT.

At the end of the Windows NT project, some developers left the company. Others were so burned out that they left the software field entirely. Recognizing this phenomenon, some experienced developers are reluctant to sign up for new projects because they know that they might once again expose themselves to lost evenings, spent weekends, and missed summers.

Developers can avoid this work pattern by adopting an engineering approach to software development. The average project spends 40–80 percent of its time correcting defects. Project teams following a software engineering approach don't create the defects in the first place, or they position themselves to eliminate the defects more quickly and easily. Eliminating 50 percent of the work is one quick way to reduce the work week from 80 hours to 40.

The commitment software developers' have to their projects as compared to their commitment to their companies is unusual. In my experience, no matter how much software developers dislike their companies, they rarely quit mid-project. Workers in other fields might say, "I hate my company. I'm going to wait until right in the middle of the project, then quit. That'll show them!" But software developers say, "I hate my company. I'm going to finish this project to show the company what they're losing, then I'll quit. That'll show them!"

Despite their lack of commitment to company, programmers do seem committed to their occupation. Many programmers feel more loyal to their colleagues at other companies than they do to their employers, and one consequence is that companies have difficulty enforcing nondisclosure agreements. I have observed that software developers routinely discuss confidential company material with colleagues who are not covered by nondisclosure agreements. In their judgment, the free exchange of information between developers is more important than any one specific company's need to protect its trade secrets. As an example of loyalty to colleagues over companies taken to the extreme, consider programmers in the Open Source movement, who advocate that all source code and related materials should be disclosed for the public good.

I think this loyalty to a project, tendency to work long hours, and high need for creativity are all related: once a programmer has visualized the software to be built, bringing the vision to life becomes paramount and the programmer feels tremendously unsettled until that can be done.

Programmers are willing to commit to something beyond themselves— to their teammates, to their projects, or to their colleagues industry-wide. This willingness to make strong occupational commitments bodes well for establishing a profession of software engineering, which can provide a constructive focus for occupational commitment.

Software Demographics

The stereotype of programmers as young men appears to have some merit too. The average software worker is significantly younger than the United States labor force. As Figure 3-1 shows, the age structure of the workforce peaks at 30–35 years old, which is about 10 years younger than the peak for other types of technical workers. The average age is 38 years old, which is younger than the average age of the United States labor force overall.

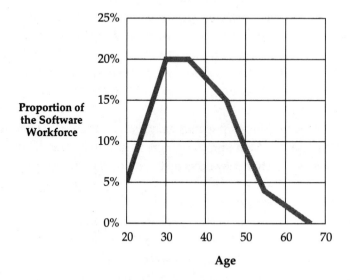

Proportion of the Software Workforce

Age

FIGURE 3-1 *The biggest group of software workers is 30–35, which is about 10 years younger than the biggest groups of workers in other technical occupations. (Source: Lowell and Burgess, "A Moving Target: Studies Try to Define the IT Workforce," 1999.)*

The majority of software developers are male. In the latest year for which data is available (1996), 72 percent of the bachelor degrees in computer and information science and 85 percent of the PhDs were awarded to men. In high school, only 17 percent of students taking the advanced placement test for computer science are female, which is the lowest of any subject.

The comparison of programmers to Pony Express riders begins to look less and less like an exaggeration (though I don't have any evidence that computer programmers are any more "wirey" than average).

Education

Many programmers go through a gradual occupational awakening. When I wrote my first small programs, I thought, "Once I get the program to compile and quit getting all these syntax errors, I'll have computer programming figured out." After I stopped having problems with syntax errors, sometimes my programs still didn't work, and the remaining problems seemed even harder to figure out than the syntax errors. I adopted a new belief, "Once I get the program debugged, I'll have computer programming figured out." That belief held true until I started creating larger programs and began having problems because the various pieces I implemented didn't work together the way I thought they would. I came to rest on a new belief, "Once I figure out how to design effectively, I'll finally have software development figured out." I created some beautiful designs, but some of them had to be changed because the requirements kept changing. At that point, I thought, "Once I figure out how to get good requirements, I'll finally have software development figured out." Somewhere along the path to learning how to get good requirements I began to realize that I might *never* get software development figured out. That realization was my first real step toward software engineering enlightenment.

Programmers take many circuitous paths to personal enlightenment, some resembling mine, some not. As I mentioned earlier in the chapter, and as Table 3-1 shows, about 60 percent of software developers have obtained bachelor's degrees or higher. According to the United Engineering Foundation, about 40 percent of all software workers obtained their degrees in software-related disciplines. About half of those who eventually obtained a software-related degree did so after first obtaining a bachelor's degree in some other subject. Another 20 percent of all software workers obtained degrees in subjects such as mathematics, engineering, English, history, or philosophy. The remaining 40 percent completed high school or some college but did not obtain a four-year degree. Universities in the United States currently award about 25,000 computer science and related degrees per year, whereas about 50,000 new software development jobs are created each year.

TABLE 3-1   SOFTWARE DEVELOPER EDUCATION

Highest Level of Education Attained	Percent of Software Developers
High school graduate or equivalent or less	10
Some college, no degree	21
Associate's degree	10
Bachelor's degree	45
Graduate degree	14

The implication of all these statistics is that a great many software developers are well educated in general but have not received any systematic training in computer science, much less in software engineering. What education they have obtained has been acquired through on-the-job training or self-study. Providing more consistent education in software engineering represents a significant opportunity to improve the level of software development practices. (I'll discuss this more in Chapter 12.)

Job Prospects

Total current employment for software workers in the United States is about 2 million. As Table 3-2 shows, jobs are divided among computer programmers, systems analysts, computer scientists, computer operators, and network administrators. (These government-statistic job titles might sound old fashioned, but they do include modern software jobs.)

TABLE 3-2   **JOB BREAKDOWN OF SOFTWARE WORKERS**

Job Title	Current Number of Software Personnel in the U.S.
Computer programmers	617,000
Systems analysts	671,000
Database administrators, computer support specialists, and other computer scientists	289,000
Computer operators/network administrators	249,000
Total	1,826,000

Job prospects for software developers in the United States are very good. According to the Bureau of Labor Statistics, computer and data processing services will be the fastest growing job category between 1996 and 2006, with a projected increase of more than 100 percent during this period. The job category in second place, health services, has a projected increase of less than 70 percent. All computer-related job categories except computer operators are expected to increase.

Worldwide, software development jobs are expected to increase as dramatically as they are increasing in the United States. Table 3-3 shows the projected increase.

TABLE 3-3   **SOFTWARE DEVELOPMENT JOBS WORLDWIDE**

Year	Total Programmers
1950	100
1960	10,000
1970	100,000
1980	2,000,000
1990	7,000,000
2000	10,000,000
2010	14,000,000
2020	21,000,000

With a 25,000 job-per-year gap between bachelor's degrees awarded and jobs created, demand for computer programmers should remain high in the United States for at least the next several years. This labor shortage has been a perennial feature of the software world at least since the mid-1960s. Software-related jobs are rated well in terms of salary, benefits, work environment, job stress, job security, and other factors. Desirable as these jobs are, programmers know that there isn't much competition for them.

Programming Heroes and Ball Hogs

Combine a shortage of workers with the common tendency to set overly optimistic schedules, and the stage is set for the programming hero. Programming heroes take on challenging assignments and write mountains of code. They work vast amounts of overtime. They become indispensable to their projects. Success, it seems, rests squarely on their shoulders.

Project managers both love and fear hero programmers because these programmers are smart, temperamental, and sometimes a little self-righteous, and because the managers don't see any way to complete projects without them. In a tight labor market, replacing them isn't an option.

Unfortunately, the reality is that, for every programming hero capable of monumental coding achievements, there are other pathological programming disasters who just don't know how to work well with others. They hoard design information and source code. They refuse to participate in technical reviews. They refuse to follow standards established by the team.

The sum total of their actions is to prevent other team members from making potentially valuable contributions. A significant number of programming heroes don't turn out to be heroes at all; they turn out to be prima donna programming ball hogs.

Individual heroics can contribute to project success, but teamwork generally contributes more than individual accomplishment does. A study at IBM found that the average programmer spends only about 30 percent of the time working alone. The rest is spent working with teammates, with customers, and on interactive activities. Another study of 31 software projects found that the greatest single contributor to overall productivity was team cohesiveness. Individual capabilities also significantly influenced productivity but were less influential than team cohesiveness.

Many people like to take on challenging projects that stretch their capabilities. Those who can test their limits, follow sound software engineering practices, and still cooperate with their teammates are the true programming heroes.

Cult of Personality

Upon examination, many aspects of the programmer personality stereotypes turn out to be accurate. The worst part of the stereotype—pathological heroism—might be due in part to industry demographics. The perennial labor shortage means that anyone with a strong enough interest in software development work can get a job as a computer programmer. The job market protects workers who become self-styled heroes.

The labor shortage contributes to increased hours for all available workers—heroes and others—which means less time for their self-education and professional development. This situation gives rise to a sort of "catch 22": we can't implement better development practices until we find the time for education and training, and we can't find the time for education and training until we implement better practices.

Working in favor of moving toward true software engineering professionalism is the fact that software developers are getting older. The longer the software field exists, the more the average age of software developers will begin to match the age of the rest of the working population. The extreme personal sacrifices that are tolerable to workers in their 20s become harder to justify as those workers marry, have children, buy homes, and move into their 30s, 40s, and 50s. As the current cohort of software workers grows older, the present hero-based approach to software development may naturally give way to an approach that relies more on working smart than on working hard. Software workers will become increasingly interested in the practices that allow them to complete their projects as promised and still be home in time for dinner.

4

Software Engineering Is Not Computer Science

---◆---

"A scientist builds in order to learn;
an engineer learns in order to build."
—Fred Brooks

---◆---

When interviewing candidates for programming jobs, one of my favorite interview questions is, "How would you describe your approach to software development?" I give them examples such as carpenter, fire fighter, architect, artist, author, explorer, scientist, and archeologist, and I invite them to come up with their own answers. Some candidates try to second-guess what I want to hear; they usually tell me they see themselves as "scientists." Hot-shot coders tell me they see themselves as commandos or swat-team members. My favorite answer came from a candidate who said, "During software design, I'm an architect. When I'm designing the user interface, I'm an artist. During construction, I'm a craftsman. And during unit testing, I'm one mean son of a bitch!"

I like to pose this question because it gets at a fundamental issue in our field: what is the best way to think of software development? Is it science? Is it art? Is it craft? Is it something else entirely?

Is vs. Should

We have a long tradition in the software field of debating whether software development is art or science. Thirty years ago, Donald Knuth began writing a seven-volume series, *The Art of Computer Programming*. The first three volumes stand at 2,200 pages, suggesting the full seven might amount to more than 5,000 pages. If that's what the *art* of computer programming looks like, I'm not sure I want to see the *science*!

People who advocate programming as art point to the aesthetic aspects of software development and argue that science does not allow for such inspiration and creative freedom. People who advocate programming as science point to the high error rates of many programs and argue that such low reliability is intolerable—creative freedom be damned. Both these views are incomplete and both ask the wrong question. Software development is art. It is science. It is craft, archeology, fire fighting, sociology, and a host of other pursuits. It is amateurish in some quarters, quasi-professional in others. It is as many different things as there are different people programming. So the proper question is not "What *is* software development currently?" but rather "What *should* professional software development be?" In my opinion, the answer to that question is clear: professional software development should be engineering. Is it? No. But should it be? Unquestionably, yes.

Engineering vs. Science

With only about 40 percent of software developers holding computer science degrees and practically none holding degrees in software engineering, we shouldn't be surprised to find people confused about the difference between software engineering and computer science. The distinction between science and engineering in software is the same as the distinction in any other field. Scientists learn what is true, how to test hypotheses, and how to extend knowledge in their fields. Engineers learn what is true, what is useful, and how to apply well-understood knowledge to solve practical problems. Scientists must keep up to date with the latest research. Engineers must be familiar with knowledge that has already proved to be reliable and effective. If you are doing science, you can afford to be narrow and specialized. If you are doing engineering, you need a broad understanding of all the factors that affect the product you are designing. Scientists don't have to be licensed because they are chiefly accountable to other scientists. Engineers do have to be licensed because they are chiefly accountable to the public. An undergraduate science education prepares students to continue their studies. An undergraduate engineering education prepares students to enter the workforce immediately after completing their studies.

Universities award computer science degrees, and they normally expect their computer science students to obtain software development jobs in which they will immediately begin solving real-world problems. Only a small fraction of computer science undergraduates go on to graduate school or research environments in which they are advancing the state of knowledge about software or computers.

This puts computer science students into a technological no-man's land. They are called scientists, but they are performing job functions that are traditionally performed by engineers without the benefit of engineering training. The effect is roughly the same as it would be if you assigned a physics PhD the task of designing electrical equipment for commercial sale. The physicist might understand the electrical principles better than the engineers he was working with, but his experience in building equipment is in creating prototypes that are used to advance the state of knowledge in a laboratory. He does not have experience or training in designing rugged, economical equipment that provides practical solutions in real-world settings. We would expect the equipment designed by the physics PhD to work but perhaps to lack some of the robustness that would make it usable or safe outside a laboratory. Or the equipment might use materials in a way that is acceptable for a single prototype but extravagantly wasteful when units are manufactured by the thousands.

Situations resembling this simple physics example occur literally thousands of times each year in software. When workers educated as computer scientists begin working on production systems, they often design and build software that is too frail for production use or that is unsafe. They focus narrowly and deeply on minor considerations to the exclusion of other considerations that are more important. They might spend two days hand-tuning a sorting algorithm instead of two hours using a code library or copying a suitable algorithm from a book. The typical computer science graduate usually needs several years of on-the-job training to accumulate enough practical knowledge to build minimally satisfactory production software without supervision. Without appropriate formal education, some software developers work their entire careers without acquiring this knowledge.

The lack of professional development isn't solely the software developer's failure. The software world has become a victim of its own success. The software job market has been growing faster than the educational infrastructure that's needed to support it, and so more than half the people holding software development jobs have been educated in subjects other than software. Employers can't require these software retreads to obtain the equivalent of an undergraduate engineering degree in their off hours. Even if they could, most of the courses available are in computer science, not software engineering. The educational infrastructure has fallen behind the industry's needs.

Beyond the Buzzword

Some people think that "software engineering" is just a buzzword that means the same thing as "computer programming." Admittedly, "software engineering" has been misused. But a term can be abused and still have a legitimate meaning.

The dictionary definition of "engineering" is the application of scientific and mathematical principles toward practical ends. That is what most programmers try to do. We apply scientifically developed and mathematically defined algorithms, functional design methods, quality-assurance methods, and other practices to develop software products and services. As David Parnas points out, in other technical fields the engineering professions were invented and given legal standing so that customers could know who was qualified to build technical products. Software customers deserve no less.

Some people think that treating software development as engineering means we'll all have to use formal methods—writing programs as mathematical proofs. Both common sense and experience tell us that that is overkill for many projects. Others object that commercial software is too dependent on changing market conditions to permit careful, time-consuming engineering.

These objections are based upon a narrow and mistaken idea of engineering. Engineering is the application of scientific principles toward *practical* ends. If the engineering isn't practical, it's bad engineering. Trying to apply formal methods to all software projects is just as bad as trying to apply code-and-fix development to all projects.

Treating software as engineering makes clearer the idea that different development goals are appropriate for different projects. When a building is designed, the construction materials must suit the building's purpose. I can build a large equipment shed to store farming vehicles from thin, uninsulated sheet metal. I wouldn't build a house the same way. But even though the house is sturdier and warmer, we wouldn't refer to the shed as being inferior to the house in any way. The shed has been designed appropriately for its intended purpose. If it had been built in the same way as the house, we might even criticize it for being "over-engineered"—a judgment implying that the designers wasted resources building the shed and that the shed was therefore poorly engineered.

In the software field, a well-run project can be managed to meet one or more of the following product objectives:

- Minimal defects

- High correctness

- Maximum user satisfaction

- Minimal response time

- Good maintainability

- Good extendibility

- High robustness

Each software project team should define the relative importance of each characteristic explicitly, and then it should conduct the project in a way that achieves the project's objectives.

In most kinds of engineering, minimizing the cost of materials is an important objective. One way that software projects differ from engineering projects is that labor costs can account for almost 100 percent of the total project cost. In other kinds of engineering, the cost of materials can contribute 50 percent or more to the total project cost. Some engineering companies report that they automatically regard projects with labor constituting more than 50 percent of project cost as high risk. Most engineering projects focus on optimizing *product* goals; design costs are relatively insignificant compared to manufacturing and production costs. Because labor cost makes up such a large part of total software project costs, software projects need to focus more on optimizing *project* goals than other kinds of engineering do. So, in addition to working toward product objectives, a software team might also work to achieve any of the following project objectives:

- Short schedule
- Predictable delivery date
- Low cost
- Small team size
- Flexibility to make mid-project feature-set changes

Each software project must strike a balance among various project and product goals. We don't want to pay $5,000 for a word processor, nor do we want one that crashes every 15 minutes (though it hasn't been all that many years since we put up with both).

Which of these specific product and project characteristics a project team emphasizes does not determine whether a project is a true "software engineering" project. Some projects need to produce software with minimal defects and near-perfect reliability—software for medical equipment, avionics, anti-lock brakes, and so on. Most people would agree that these projects are an appropriate domain for full-up software engineering. Other projects need to deliver their software with adequate reliability but with low costs and short schedules. Are these properly the domain of software engineering? One informal definition of engineering is "doing for a dime what anyone can do for a dollar." Lots of software projects today are doing for a dollar what any good software engineer could do for a dime. Economical development is also the domain of software engineering.

Today's pervasive reliance on code-and-fix development—and the cost and schedule overruns that go with it—is not the result of a software engineering calculation but rather of too little education and training in software engineering practices.

The Right Questions

Software development as it's commonly practiced today doesn't look much like engineering, but it could. Once we stop asking the wrong question, "*Is software development really engineering?*" and start asking the right question, "*Should* professional software development be engineering?" we can start answering the really interesting questions. What is software engineering's core body of knowledge? How should professional software engineers be educated? Should professional software engineers be certified or licensed? Should software companies be licensed? Should the software itself be licensed? And, perhaps the most interesting question of all: what will the software industry look like after all these questions have been answered?

II

PROSPECTING

5

After the Gold Rush

---◆---

*"The root of all superstition is that men observe
when a thing hits but not when it misses."*
—*Francis Bacon*

---◆---

In January 1848, James Marshall discovered gold in California's American River near a mill he was building for John Sutter. At first Marshall and Sutter dismissed the pea-sized nuggets as a nuisance; they believed the attention that gold would bring would spoil Sutter's plans to build an agricultural empire. But within months word spread, and by 1849 thousands of men and a handful of women from around the world had contracted gold rush fever. They headed to California to make their fortunes in what became known as the California gold rush. The rush west created a new economy driven by high-risk entrepreneurialism and fueled by the dream of striking it rich. Precious few 49ers actually realized that dream during the gold rush days, but the dream lives on in many modern software companies and individual software developers.

The California gold rush was unique in that the gold was found in riverbeds instead of embedded in hard rock. That meant that, at first, anyone with a tin pan and an entrepreneurial spirit had a chance to make a fortune. But by mid 1849, most of the easy gold had been found, which meant that a typical miner spent 10 hours a day in ice cold water, digging, sifting, and washing. As time passed, this backbreaking work yielded less and less gold. There were occasional lucky strikes well into the 1850s, which provided just enough good news to encourage thousands to keep digging. Most failed every day, but they kept on for years.

After the early days of the gold rush, miners had to use more advanced techniques to extract gold. By the early 1850s, a single miner could no longer work a claim by himself. He needed the help of other people and technology. At first, miners banded together informally to build dams, reroute rivers, and extract the gold. But soon more capital-intensive techniques were needed, and the informal groups of miners were replaced by corporations. By the mid 1850s, most of the miners who remained were corporate employees rather than individual entrepreneurs.

Software Gold Rushes

The advent of a major new technology often means the beginning of what I think of as a "software gold rush." Companies and individual entrepreneurs rush into new technology areas, hoping that a little bit of hard work will produce a product that will make them wealthy. I've personally seen software gold rushes with the advent of the IBM PC and the MS-DOS operating system, the migration from MS-DOS to Microsoft Windows, and the growth of Internet computing. More new-technology gold rushes will undoubtedly follow.

Gold rush software development is characterized by high-risk, high-reward development practices. Few companies establish a competitive presence in the marketplace during the early days of a new technology, and many of the new-technology gold nuggets—successful new products—seem to be lying on the ground, waiting for anyone with the right mix of innovation and initiative to pick them up. Software 49ers rush into the new technology, hoping to stake their claim before anyone else does. The typical gold rushers are two guys working in a garage, legendary dynamic duos such as Bill Gates and Paul Allen of Microsoft, Steve Jobs and Steve Wozniak of Apple Computer, and Bob Frankston and Dan Bricklin of Visicalc.

The practices employed by software developers with gold rush fever are usually associated with hacking rather than engineering: informal processes, long hours, little documentation, bare-bones quality assurance—in other words, hero-based code-and-fix development. These practices require little training and low overhead, and they expose projects to a high risk of failure.

The odds of striking it rich during a software gold rush are about as good as they were during the California gold rush—for every success story, there are hundreds or even thousands of projects that go bust. But these small failures aren't nearly as interesting as the huge successes, and so we don't hear very much about them. Two guys who work hard and don't strike it rich aren't a very good news story, unless by chance there's something interesting about their garage.

As with the California gold rush, software projects that are run with hero-based development in gold rush periods are successful from time to time. At a personal level, the odds of striking it rich, such as they are, are probably better in an entrepreneurial gold rush environment than they are in a post–gold rush environment. The gold rush projects are so enormously lucrative when they do succeed however, that they convince software developers that high-risk practices can work, and thus the rare but widely publicized successes spread gold rush fever and help to keep hero-based practices alive.

Post–Gold Rush Development

Post–gold rush software development is characterized by more methodical, lower-risk, capital-intensive development practices. Projects use larger teams, rely on more formal processes, adhere to more standards (compatibility with legacy code, industry-wide protocols, and so on), and work with much larger code bases. The emphasis is less on rushing software to market quickly and more on reliability, interoperability, usability, and other software engineering considerations that hardly matter during a gold rush but that matter a lot after a technology matures.

Gold rush–style development practices have even lower odds of working in a post–gold rush phase than they did during the risky gold rush phase. In the early days of a new technology, there are few established players or products. The technological barriers to entry are low, and early products can be small, unpolished, and unreliable and still succeed. As with the California gold rush, fewer people and less capital are needed to stake a claim during the early days of a new technology. The first version of Microsoft Word for the Macintosh was a gold rush product that consisted of just 153,000 lines of code. Two guys in a garage have a chance to compete against the major corporations when a successful product can be built with 153,000 lines of code. As the technology matures, however, the easy gold runs out, and successful companies have to compete on the basis of more capital-intensive projects.

One of the most damaging mistakes that successful gold rush companies make is to persist in using gold rush development approaches as the technology matures and their projects scale up. To compete successfully in the post–gold rush phase, the successful project needs to do a lot more than simply multiply the number of guys and get a bigger garage.

Post–gold rush customers are more demanding. Gold rush customers are what Geoffrey Moore, author of *Crossing the Chasm*, calls "innovators" and "early adopters." They tend to be technologically savvy, drawn to new technologies, and forgiving of the rough edges that go along with them. Gold rush products can be much less polished than the products that come later and still be successful. Post–gold rush customers are what Moore calls "early majority," "late majority," and "laggards." They are risk averse and want polished products that work reliably. This demand sets a higher bar for post–gold rush products. The current version of Microsoft Word for Windows, a post–gold rush product, consists of more than 5 million lines of code.

One surprising implication of gold rush dynamics is that the companies that are successful during one gold rush are likely to fail during the next gold rush. The archetypal post–gold rushers are the companies that became established during an earlier gold rush. These companies repeat Marshall and Sutter's mistake of seeing new-technology gold as a nuisance that will interfere with their well-laid plans for extracting maximum value from the claims they staked during the last gold rush. Examples of companies that were slow to pick up new-technology gold nuggets include IBM during the early days of PC-DOS; Lotus during the early days of Windows; and Microsoft during the early dawn of the Internet, although Microsoft recovered from its early mistakes. The most compelling example in modern computing has to be Xerox. Many of the fundamental ideas of modern desktop computing were invented at Xerox's Palo Alto Research Center, including the GUI, the mouse, and the Ethernet. But Xerox was so busy trying not to lose the copy machine war that it lost the computing war without ever really entering it.

Other post–gold rush companies are just too bloated to compete effectively in gold rush markets. The overhead necessary to sell to "early majority" and "late majority" customers isn't needed during a gold rush. In a gold rush market, you can cut your products to the bone and still do well with the innovators and early adopters who count the most in those markets.

We'll undoubtedly see this boom and bust pattern repeated during whatever technology cycle follows the Internet. Some of the companies that had the greatest successes in the early days of the Internet—Netscape, Yahoo, Amazon.com—will miss the next wave. Only time will tell which will successfully navigate the next great transition.

The Sense and Nonsense of Gold Rush Economics

From a macroeconomic viewpoint, thousands of individual software developers taking on entrepreneurial risk voluntarily—with a few lucky entrepreneurs striking it rich and the rest chalking up their losses to experience—is tremendously beneficial. No one but the individual entrepreneurs pays for the failures, and everyone has a chance to benefit from buying and using the products that succeed. But how can an individual company harness this dynamic? What company could possibly afford to fund thousands of individual entrepreneurs during a gold rush phase just to find the one or two that successfully develop new gold rush technology? Even companies with extensive research facilities such as AT&T, Microsoft, and Xerox can't afford to fund thousands of projects in each new technology area. No company can afford it, which is one reason that software company acquisitions during a gold rush phase are more sensible than they at first appear. Some industry observers thought Microsoft was crazy to pay $130 million to acquire Vermeer Technology, original creators of FrontPage, when Vermeer had only about $10 million in annual revenue. But from the entrepreneurial gold rush point of view, paying $130 million for the one success in a thousand is a cheap alternative to funding a thousand dead-end entrepreneurial experiments internally.

Scaling Up and Scaling Down

Post–gold rush software engineering practices have unequivocally proved their worth on large projects. (Doubters can turn to Chapter 7.) They also have a lot to offer smaller projects. Larry Constantine describes an Australian Computer Society Software Challenge, in which three-person teams had to develop and deliver a 200 function-point application in six hours. This is a significant challenge, equivalent to writing about 20,000 lines of code in a traditional third-generation language or about 5,000 lines of code in a visual programming language.

A team from the accounting firm Ernst and Young decided to follow a formal development methodology—a scaled-down version of their regular methodology—complete with staged activities and intermediate deliverables. Their approach included careful requirements analysis and design. Many of their competitors dived straight into coding, and for the first couple of hours the team from Ernst and Young lagged behind.

But by midday they had developed a commanding lead. At the end of the day the team from Ernst and Young lost, but not because their systematic approach had failed. They lost because they accidentally overwrote some of their working files, squandering their afternoon work and delivering less functionality than they had demonstrated at lunch time.

Would the team from Ernst and Young have won had it not been for the configuration-management snafu? The answer is "yes." They reappeared a few months later at another rapid-development face-off—this time with version control and backup—and they won. Their success was achieved not by stripping down their earlier approach but by identifying weaknesses in their old process and making improvements.

This general value of applying systematic process improvement within small organizations was confirmed by a Software Engineering Institute study which found that the success rate of process improvement programs in organizations with fewer than 50 software developers was just as good as it was in larger organizations. Moreover, small organizations had fewer of the problems that inhibited success in larger organizations such as organizational politics and turf guarding.

Back to the Gold Rush

Gold rush software projects might be inherently risky, but the use of haphazard software development practices has made them riskier than they need to be. Developers working on gold rush projects have been saddled for decades with the methodological equivalents of tin pans and shovels. The result is that much of their insights, ideas, and innovations are needlessly lost, just as the Ernst and Young team's work was needlessly lost due to lack of source code control.

Systematic approaches to software engineering are necessary for post–gold rush projects to succeed; they are equally useful for projects still in the gold rush stage. What would have happened if the original designers of Visicalc, Lotus 123, MacOS, the Mosaic web browser, and other groundbreaking products had overwritten their working files? How many innovative products have we never heard of because their developers actually did overwrite their working files? And how many have succumbed to more subtle errors?

During a gold rush, you can be terribly sloppy and not very skilled and still make a fortune (if you're lucky). After a gold rush, you have to be more disciplined and more skilled just to break even. The entrepreneurial buzz a person gets from participating in a gold rush project is one of life's great thrills, but there's no conflict between entrepreneurial energy and the use of effective software development practices. By examining the practices that work well after a gold rush, you can gain insight into practices that work well even on projects with gold rush fever.

Tera was a gold rush.

6
Engineering a Profession

---◆---

"Engineering can provide a life of genuine satisfaction in many ways, especially through ministering in a practical manner to the needs and welfare of mankind."
—*Vannevar Bush*

---◆---

"There is no essential difference between the artist and the craftsman. The artist is an exalted craftsman. In rare moments of inspiration, moments beyond the control of his will, the grace of heaven may cause his work to blossom into art. But proficiency in his craft is essential to every artist. Therein lies a source of creative imagination."
—*Walter Gropius*

---◆---

Engineers are saddled with much the same stereotype as computer programmers—they are regarded as boring and dull. And yet these boring and dull engineers are responsible for some of the most exciting developments in the world today. Science gets the credit for many technological miracles that truly belong to engineering. Putting a man on the moon, view-ing the outer reaches of space from the Hubble space telescope, flying on modern jet aircraft, driving by car from coast to coast, connecting to Inter-net sites throughout the world, enjoying theater-quality video presentations at home—these technological miracles are all predominately engineering accomplishments, the practical application of scientific principles.

Need for Engineering

Historically, professional engineering has been established in response to threats to public safety. Although we take the safety of modern bridges for granted, in the 1860s American bridges were failing at the rate of 25 or more per year. Bridge failures and the loss of life they caused precipitated crea-tion of a stricter engineering approach to bridge design and construction. In Canada, engineering folklore holds that the collapse of the Quebec City bridge in 1907 catalyzed establishment of higher standards in all branches of Canadian engineering, which is symbolized today in the iron ring cer-emony, which engineers go through at graduation time. (I'll describe the significance of the iron ring in more detail in Chapter 10.) As I mentioned in the Introduction, engineers in Texas were licensed only after a boiler ex-plosion in an elementary school killed more than 300 children.

Engineering differs from other professions in that doctors, dentists, public accountants, lawyers, and so on generally provide their services to specific individuals or, in some cases, to specific corporations. Engineers tend to *design things* rather than provide services to individuals. Their re-sponsibility is more often to society than to specific individuals. In this sense, software developers are more like engineers than they are like other kinds of professionals.

Any reader of the *Forum on Risks to the Public in the Use of Computers and Related Systems* knows the potential exists for a software disaster that will galvanize public opinion in favor of a higher standard of professional con-duct. Software has already been responsible for many multimillion-dollar losses, ranging from the ridiculous to the deadly. Tsutomu Shimomura parked at a San Diego airport parking lot on February 29, 1992. When he returned six days later, his parking bill was $3,771. The parking software didn't rec-ognize February 29 as a valid date. In January 1990 approximately 5 million telephone calls were blocked over a nine-hour period because of a software error. The first space shuttle launch was delayed for two days because of a subtle programming error. The Mariner I space probe to Venus was lost because of an error in transcribing a guidance equation into software. In London, a computer dispatch system for ambulances was placed into operation before it was ready, collapsed completely, and caused delays as long as 11 hours; as many as 20 deaths were attributed to the collapse of the new system. Iran Air flight 655 was shot down by the USS Vincennes' Aegis system in 1988, killing 290 people. The error was initially attributed to operator error, but later some experts attributed the incident to the poor design of Aegis's user interface.

Only time will tell what software disaster will play the role of the Quebec City bridge or Texas elementary school boiler. But have no doubt: if poor software development practices continue on their current path, they will eventually produce a disaster (or set of related disasters) that galvanizes public opinion in favor of tougher software industry standards.

Engineering and Art

Engineering's use of mathematics and science exposes it to the criticism that it is dry—that it saps the artistic elements out of the structures it creates. The same criticism has been applied to software engineering. How true is this criticism? Does engineering exclude aesthetics?

Far from being antithetical to aesthetics, engineering is largely concerned with all aspects of design, including aesthetic aspects. Its designs aren't just limited to shapes and colors. Engineers design everything from electronic circuits to load-bearing beams to vehicles that land on the moon. As Samuel C. Florman says in *Existential Pleasures of Engineering,* "Creative design is the central mission of the professional engineer."

Consider a comparison of two well-known buildings, the Reims Cathedral and the Sydney Opera House. The Reims Cathedral, shown in Figure 6-1, was completed about 1290; the Sydney Opera House in 1973. The Reims Cathedral was designed to use materials whose properties were understood (more or less) at the time.

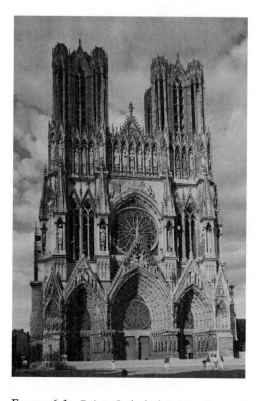

FIGURE 6-1   *Reims Cathedral, Reims, France. An example of art without very well developed engineering.*

The Sydney Opera House was constructed 700 years after the Reims Cathedral. As you can see in Figure 6-2, it's stylistically quite different from the Reims Cathedral. Its architects used modern materials such as steel and reinforced concrete, and they employed engineering techniques including computer modeling to determine how little material could safely be used.

Which building you prefer is a matter of taste, but which building can actually be built is a matter of engineering. It would be possible for modern builders to construct another Reims cathedral, but it would not have been possible for 13th century builders to construct a Sydney Opera House. The reason the Sydney Opera House could not be constructed by builders in the thirteenth century was not a lack of art but a lack of engineering. We've all seen ugly buildings in which artistic considerations lost a battle with engineering economy, or in which aesthetics appear not to have been considered at all. Engineering without art can be ugly, but art without engineering may be impossible. Engineering does not constrain artistic possibilities. The *lack* of engineering constrains artistic possibilities.

FIGURE 6-2   *Sydney Opera House, Sydney, Australia. An example of the dependence of art upon engineering.*

So it is with modern software systems. The level of engineering prowess determines how large a system can be built successfully, how easy it will be to use, how fast it will operate, how many errors it will contain, and how well it will cooperate with other systems. Software includes many aesthetic elements, and software developers have no lack of artistic ambition. What we in the software industry sometimes lack is the engineering technique that enables us to realize some of our grandest aesthetic aspirations.

Maturation of Engineering Disciplines

The response to disasters in existing engineering fields has been to professionalize engineering practices. Of course, a full-fledged engineering discipline can't simply be willed into existence overnight. Mary Shaw at Carnegie Mellon University has identified how fields progress on their way to professional engineering. Figure 6-3 summarizes this maturation.

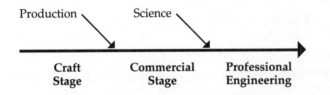

FIGURE 6-3   *The progression of a discipline from craft to professional engineering. (Source: adapted from Shaw, "Prospects for an Engineering Discipline of Software," 1990.)*

In the craft stage, good work is performed by talented amateurs. Craftsmen use intuition and skill to create their widgets, whether their widgets are bridges, electric equipment, or computer programs. Some of their work is intended for sale to the public, but most is created solely for their own use. They have little or no concept of large-scale production for external sale. Craftsmen tend to make extravagant use of available materials. In the craft stage, a field progresses haphazardly; no systematic way to educate or train other craftsmen in the use of the most effective techniques is in place.

Civil engineering (aqueduct and bridge construction) in first century Rome was a discipline in its craft stage, as was early computing in the 1950s and 1960s. Many software projects today still make extravagant use of available resources (staff time) and operate at the craft level.

At some point, the demand for the widgets increases beyond what isolated craftsmen can provide, and demand for greater production begins to influence the discipline. As the folklore of a craft becomes better understood, it's codified into written heuristics and procedural rules. In the commercial stage, workers more carefully define the resources needed to support production. This stage is marked by a stronger economic orientation, and cost of goods may become an issue. Practitioners are trained to ensure consistent quality of the widgets they produce. Production procedures are systematically refined by changing different parameters to see what works and what doesn't.

The Reims Cathedral was built at a time when civil engineering was in its commercial stage. In software, many commercial-stage organizations achieve respectable levels of quality and productivity by making use of carefully selected, well-trained personnel. They rely on familiar practices and change them incrementally in pursuit of better products and better project performance.

Some of the problems encountered by commercial production can't be solved via trial and error, and, if the economic stakes are high enough, a corresponding science will develop. As the science matures, it develops theories that contribute to commercial practice, and this is the point at which true professional engineering practice emerges. Progress arises from application of scientific principles as well as from practical experimentation. The practitioners working in the field at this point must be well educated in both the theory and practice of their profession.

A Science for Software Development

Software science has been lagging behind commercial software development for years. Extremely large software systems were developed in the 1950s and 1960s, including the Sage missile defense system, the Sabre airline-reservation system, and IBM's OS/360 operating system. Commercial development of these large systems proceeded much faster than supporting research did, but practical applications advancing faster than science is not unprecedented in engineering. The airfoil wing section that allows airplanes to fly was invented just after it had been "proved" that no machine heavier than air could fly. The development of thermodynamics followed the invention of the steam engine. When John Roebling designed the Brooklyn Bridge in the 1860s, the strength of steel cables was not well understood, and so he designed different parts of the bridge with safety margins ranging as high as 6-to-1. This safety margin was an engineering judgment made in lieu of better theoretical knowledge.

The sciences that support software development aren't as well defined as the physics that supports civil engineering. In fact they aren't even considered "natural science." They are what Herbert Simon calls "sciences of the artificial"—the knowledge areas of computer science, mathematics, psychology, sociology, and management science. A few software organizations regularly apply theories from these areas to their projects, but we are a long way from seeing universal application of these sciences of the artificial to software projects. But are we really asking software science to provide the right things?

For many classes of programs—inventory management systems, payroll programs, general ledger software, operating systems, database management software, language compilers (the list is nearly endless)—the same basic systems have been written so many times that you'd think they shouldn't require as much unique design effort as they seem to need. Mary Shaw points out that in mature engineering fields, routine design involves solving familiar problems and reusing large portions of prior solutions. Often these "solutions" are codified in the form of equations, analytical models, or pre-built components. Unique design challenges do present themselves from time to time, but the bread and butter of engineering is the application of routine design practices to familiar problems.

The software world is still in the process of capturing many of its "solutions" in ways that are useful to the average practitioner. Many software project artifacts are reusable, and many of them have more potential to improve quality and productivity than the most commonly reused artifact—source code—does. Following is a short list of some potentially reusable project artifacts. However, at present, few of these project artifacts have been packaged into a form that the average organization can readily apply.

- Architectures and software design procedures
- Design patterns
- Estimates and estimation procedures
- Organizational structures, team structures, and management procedures
- Planning data, project plans, and planning procedures
- Post-project reports and project-review procedures
- Requirements and requirements engineering procedures
- Software configuration management procedures
- Source code, construction procedures, and integration procedures
- Technical review procedures
- Test plans, test cases, test data, and test procedures
- User interface elements and user interface design procedures

Science has not yet provided the field of software engineering with a set of equations that describe how to run a project successfully, or that describe how to produce successful software products. Perhaps it never will. But science doesn't necessarily have to consist of formulas and mathematics. In *The Structure of Scientific Revolutions*, Thomas Kuhn points out that a scientific paradigm can consist of a set of solved problems. Reusable software project artifacts are a set of solved problems—solved requirements problems, design problems, planning problems, management problems, and so on.

The Call of Engineering

Arthur C. Clarke said that any sufficiently advanced technology is indistinguishable from magic. Software technology is sufficiently advanced, and the general public is mystified by it. The public doesn't understand the safety risks or the financial risks posed by software products. As high priests of powerful magic, software developers need to use the technology wisely.

Engineering may be regarded as boring in some quarters but, boring or not, engineering is a better model for software than magic is. The engineering approach to design and construction has a track record of all but eliminating some of the most serious risks to public safety and of supporting some of the most elevating expressions of the human spirit. Concerned software developers have a responsibility to ensure that software rises to the level of engineering. In the short term, software engineering practice needs to be patched up enough to prevent further software disasters. In the long term, software engineering practice needs to be elevated to a level at which it can support the next generation of technological miracles.

7

*P*tolemaic
*R*easoning

---◆---

"All models are wrong; some models are useful."
—*George Box*

---◆---

"Knowledge itself is power."
—*Francis Bacon*

---◆---

A while back I gave a talk titled "A Tale of Two Projects." My objective was to provide a glimpse of what an engineering approach to developing software looks like. I argued that good software organizations often succeed on complex, high-risk projects because they use effective software development practices, and poor organizations often fail on simple, low-risk projects because they use poor practices. The talk was generally well received, but one person's evaluation said this: "An excellent example of the kind of static, linear, Ptolemaic reasoning that ignores the dynamics and complexities of real software projects."

In case you've forgotten your grammar school science, Ptolemy was an astronomer who lived about 100 A.D. and believed that the sun revolved around the earth. His theory was replaced in 1543 when Copernicus theorized that the earth revolved around the sun. The attendee was saying that the approach I recommended was a sun-moves-around-the-earth approach—either that, or that my ideas were 400 years out of date!

Copernicus replaced Ptolemy's theory when he discovered observational data that Ptolemy's theory could not account for. Similarly, observational data from real-world software projects strongly supports the efficacy of the development practices I described, these particular comments notwithstanding.

Overview of the SW-CMM

The practices I was describing were loosely based on the Capability Maturity Model for Software (SW-CMM), developed by the Software Engineering Institute (SEI). The SW-CMM was originally proposed in 1987 and is currently the best known and most effective approach to systematic organizational improvement. The SW-CMM classifies software organizations into five levels:

◆ *Level 1: Initial* Software development is chaotic. Projects tend to run over budget and behind schedule. Organizational knowledge is contained only in the minds of individual programmers; when a programmer leaves an organization, so does the knowledge. Success depends largely on the contributions of individual "hero" programmers of the kind described in Chapter 3. These organizations tend to use code-and-fix development. Organizations are at this level by default unless they've deliberately adopted more effective approaches.

◆ *Level 2: Repeatable* Basic project management practices are established on a project-by-project basis, and the organization ensures that they are followed. Project success no longer depends solely on specific individuals. The strength of an organization at this level depends on its repeated experience with similar projects. The organization may falter when faced with new tools, methods, or kinds of software.

◆ *Level 3: Defined*   The software organization adopts standardized technical and management processes across the organization, and individual projects tailor the standard process to their specific needs. A group within the organization is assigned responsibility for software process activities. The organization establishes a training program to ensure that managers and technical staff have appropriate knowledge and skills to work at this level. The organization has moved well beyond code-and-fix development, and it routinely delivers software on time and within budget.

◆ *Level 4: Managed*   Project outcomes are highly predictable. The process is stable enough that causes of variation can be identified and addressed. The organization collects project data in an organization-wide database to evaluate the effectiveness of different processes. All projects follow organization-wide process-measurement standards so that the data they produce can be meaningfully analyzed and compared.

◆ *Level 5: Optimizing*   The focus of the whole organization is on continuous, proactive identification and dissemination of process improvements. The organization varies its processes, measures the results of the variations, and diffuses beneficial variations as new standards. The organization's quality assurance focus is on defect prevention through identification and elimination of root causes.

The underlying principle of the SW-CMM can be attributed loosely to Conway's Law: the structure of a computer program reflects the structure of the organization that built it. Chaotic organizations produce chaotic software. Organizations that hire programming heroes, give them lots of autonomy, and set them loose to create coding miracles produce software that is alternately brilliant and erratic. Organizations bloated with inefficient processes produce piggy, sluggish software. And, presumably, efficient, optimizing organizations produce finely tuned, highly satisfactory software.

The software industry has been making progress under the guidance provided by the SW-CMM. As Figure 7-1 shows, in 1991, of 129 organizations assessed, only about 20 percent were performing at levels better than Level 1.

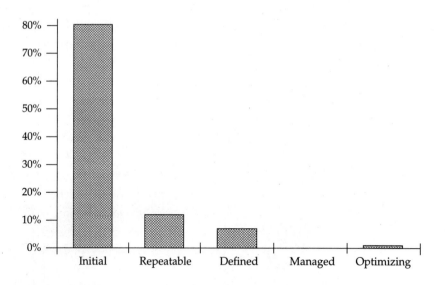

FIGURE 7-1   *Assessment profile of organizations that have been assessed using the SW-CMM as of 1991. (Source: SEI, "Process Maturity Profile of the Software Community 1998 Year End Update," 1999.)*

As Figure 7-2 shows, in 1998, of 951 organizations assessed, almost 50 percent were performing at better than Level 1.

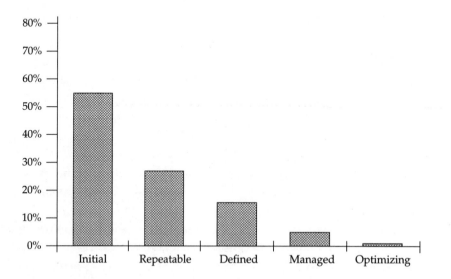

FIGURE 7-2   *Assessment profile of organizations that have been assessed using the SW-CMM as of 1998. (Source: SEI, "Process Maturity Profile of the Software Community 1998 Year End Update," 1999.)*

The trend shown by these two graphs is encouraging, but only a small fraction of all the software organizations in North America have been assessed, and I think it's safe to assume that those organizations still look a lot more like the SEI's 1991 profile than its 1998 profile—in other words, that about 75 percent of all organizations are still operating at Level 1.

Effectiveness of the SW-CMM

The seminar attendee implied that my systematic approach wouldn't work on real projects. Industry data says otherwise. An in-depth study of 13 organizations by the SEI found that the typical (median) organization engaged in SW-CMM improvement experienced a productivity gain of 35 percent per year, a schedule reduction of 19 percent per year, a reduction in post-release defect reports of 39 percent per year, and a business value of their investment in organizational improvement of about 5 to 1.

The gains experienced by the best organizations were even better. The organization with the strongest productivity gains improved 58 percent per year for four years, for a total compounded gain of more than 500 percent. The best schedule reduction was 23 percent per year for six years, for a total compounded reduction of 91 percent. The best long-term quality improvement was a reduction in post-release defect reports of 39 percent per year for nine years, for a total compounded reduction of 99 percent. Two organizations achieved short-term defect reductions of 70 percent or more in less than two years. These results are summarized in Table 7-1.

TABLE 7-1 **RESULTS OF SW-CMM PROCESS IMPROVEMENT EFFORTS**

Factor	Median Improvement	Best Sustained Improvement
Productivity	35% per year	58% per year
Schedule	19% per year	23% per year
Post-release defect reports	39% per year	39% per year*
Business value of organizational improvement	5 to 1	8.8 to 1

*   The median and sustained values here are the same because the highest defect-reduction results were counted as short-term improvements rather than as sustained improvements.

Organizations that are hooked on code-and-fix development tend to think there is a tradeoff between low defect count and productivity. But as I mentioned in Chapter 2, much of the cost on a code-and-fix project arises from unplanned defect-correction work. The results in this table confirm that no tradeoff exists for most organizations. Focus on preventing defects, and you'll also get shorter schedules and higher productivity.

Are these results attainable by average organizations? The answer is clearly "yes." As Figure 7-3 shows, the SEI studied 132 organizations that were trying to improve their SW-CMM rating from Level 1 to Level 2 or from Level 2 to Level 3. Seventy-five percent improved from Level 1 to Level 2 in 3.5 years or less, and the median time was just over two years. Seventy-five percent improved from Level 2 to Level 3 in 2 years or less, and the median time was about a year and a half. Organizations that make a serious commitment to SW-CMM–style improvement typically improve substantially, and quickly too.

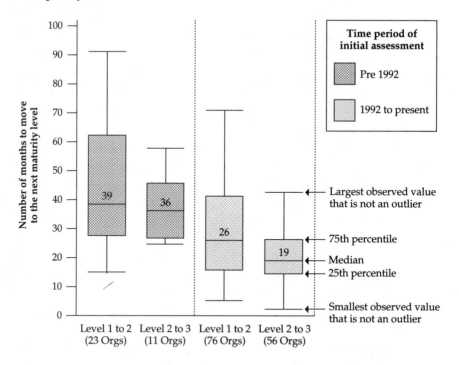

FIGURE 7-3 *Experience of organizations moving from one SW-CMM maturity level to the next. (Source: adapted from SEI, "Process Maturity Profile of the Software Community 1998 Year End Update," 1999.)*

An interesting implication of the data shown in Figure 7-3 is that process improvement is occurring significantly faster today than it did from 1987 to 1992. Considering that the SW-CMM was launched in 1987, I don't think that development is very surprising. The SEI was still working out the kinks in the model during the first five years. Today, the SEI knows better how to help organizations, which supports more rapid improvements.

All the Risk You Can Handle

My Ptolemaic seminar attendee said my approach ignored the dynamics of real projects, and other people have claimed that the SW-CMM makes organizations risk averse. Organizations become bureaucratic and conservative, the claim goes, which hurts their competitiveness. How does the industry experience bear this out?

In Level 1 organizations, less than half of the respondents to one survey said their management was willing to take on "moderate" or "substantial" risk. In Level 3 organizations, almost 80 percent of the respondents said their management was willing to take on that much risk.

This relationship between process effectiveness and ability to take on risk was demonstrated by the Cheyenne Mountain ATAMS project. The ATAMS project team committed to complete the project for one-fifth the cost and in one-half the time of the best available estimate. In the end, they delivered the software one month ahead of schedule and within budget. Eighteen months after release, only two defects had been discovered in the software, and both were easily corrected. The project team's success on this high-risk project resulted from carefully managing requirements, using formal inspections on their designs and code, and practicing active risk management.

The effect of organizational improvement on risk taking is the opposite of what some people think. By reducing exposure to unnecessary risks—the kind of risks Fred Brooks might call "accidental" rather than "essential"—the organization with sophisticated processes in place is in a better position to take on calculated, voluntary risks than less sophisticated organizations, which are overwhelmed by involuntary risks assaulting them from all sides.

Who Uses the SW-CMM?

Since 1987, more than 1,000 organizations have had their capabilities assessed, and 5,000 projects have had their results reported to the SEI. More than half of the organizations participating in SW-CMM improvement are commercial software houses or in-house development groups representing industries including finance, insurance, real estate, retail sales, construction, transportation, communications, public utilities, industrial machinery, electronic equipment, and medical instruments. About a quarter develop software under contract for the United States government. About 15 percent are military organizations or government agencies. The organizations' sizes vary widely. About half have fewer than 100 software personnel. About a quarter have more than 200, and about a quarter have less than 50.

The Myth of Soulless Software Development

One of the common objections to organizational improvement is that it imposes creativity-limiting bureaucracy. This is reminiscent of the old objection that engineering and art are incompatible. It is possible to create an oppressive environment in which programmer creativity and business goals are placed at odds, just as it is possible to create ugly buildings. But it is just as possible to set up an environment in which software developer satisfaction and business goals are in harmony, and industry data bears this out. Of people who were surveyed about the effects of the SW-CMM, 84 percent disagreed or strongly disagreed with the claim that SW-CMM–based improvement made their organizations more rigid or bureaucratic.

Organizations that have focused on organizational improvement have found that effective processes support creativity and morale. In a survey of about 50 organizations, only 20 percent of the people in Level 1 organizations rated their staff morale as good or excellent The responses were consistent across managers, developers responsible for organizational improvement, and senior technical staff members. In organizations rated at Level 2, the proportion of people who rated their staff morale as good or excellent jumped to 50 percent. And in organizations rated at Level 3, 60 percent of the people rated their morale as good or excellent.

These summary statistics are confirmed by in-depth analysis of organizations that have achieved the highest process effectiveness ratings. A survey at Ogden Air Logistics Center, one of the first organizations to be assessed at SW-CMM Level 5, found that software workers were enthusiastic about the changes brought about by their eight-year improvement effort. Respondents did feel that the Level 5 processes constrained the way they could perform their work, but the constraint was seen as an inevitable side effect of becoming more effective and wasn't considered to be negative. Software workers felt that it was much easier to perform their work than it had been before organizational improvement. The vast majority felt that they had more input into project planning and control. Every survey respondent felt that the SW-CMM initiative had been a positive influence.

The on-board shuttle software group at NASA's Johnson Space Flight Center is another organization that has been assessed at Level 5. You won't find mounds of pizza boxes, pyramids of Coca Cola cans, rock-climbing walls, skateboard parks, or any of the other trappings found in more "hip" software organizations. The emphasis is not on playing games; it is on making perfect software. The work is exciting, but it is not all-consuming. The space shuttle group generally works 8 to 5. In an industry dominated by males, about half of the shuttle software group is female.

People who leave such high-performance groups are sometimes shocked by how inefficient the average organization is. One person left the Johnson Space Flight Center for a more entrepreneurial environment, only to return a few months later. He commented that the company he went to paid lip service to developing software effectively, but their approach was really code-and-fix development. Far from finding high maturity environments limiting, people in those environments find that they can achieve levels of productivity and quality that are simply not possible in lower maturity environments. The ATAMS project described earlier used highly structured work practices that some developers might find restrictive, but the ATAMS team members said they felt the practices brought out everyone's best performance. They said they would be reluctant to develop software without them.

A View of the Best

One indicator of how much control an organization has over its projects is the accuracy of its estimates. A Standish Group survey of more than 8,000 business systems projects found that the average project overran its planned budget by more than 100 percent. The level of estimation error reported in this survey is consistent with other industry findings.

Figure 7-4 shows the results of a study of United States Air Force projects at different SW-CMM levels. Each point below 100 percent represents a project that overran its budget. Each point above 100 percent represents a project that finished under budget.

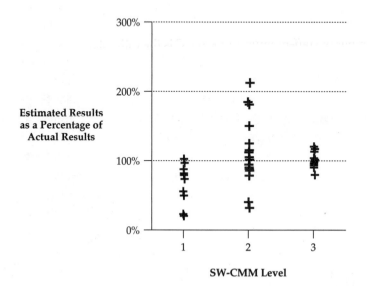

FIGURE 7-4   *As organizations progress to the upper levels of the SW-CMM, they gain more control over their project estimates, which is indicative of more control generally. (Source: adapted from Lawlis, Flowe, and Thordahl, "A Correlational Study of the CMM and Software Development Performance," 1995.)*

As you can see from the figure, organizations at SW-CMM Level 1 routinely overran their projects' budgets—in other words, they routinely underestimated their projects' costs. Organizations at Level 2 spread their estimation error more evenly between overestimation and underestimation, but the estimation error was still commonly 100 percent or more. At Level 3, overruns and underruns become equally common, and the estimation accuracy was much improved. Based on what's shown in Figure 7-4, if you were a client evaluating vendor bids from an organization at Level 1, an organization at Level 2, and an organization at Level 3, which bid would you believe?

Further examination of estimation practices holds out an interesting process-improvement carrot. Most organizations find that as their projects become larger, each team member becomes less productive. In contrast with

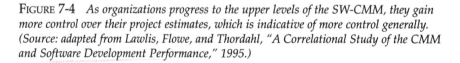

the economies of scale experienced in other kinds of work, software projects usually experience *dis*economies of scale.

Organizations that do systematic estimation use formulas like this one to estimate their software project effort:

$$Effort = 2.45 * KSLOC^{1.15}$$

Effort is the number of staff-months and *KSLOC* is the estimated number of lines of code in thousands. The numbers 2.45 and 1.15 are derived by calibration using data from projects that the organization has already completed. The values of 2.45 and 1.15 are values for typical organizations. The specific value of the exponent (1.15) is significant because it means that larger projects require disproportionately more effort than smaller projects.

NASA's Software Engineering Laboratory (SEL) is a notable exception. The SEL was the first organization to receive the IEEE Computer Society's award for software process achievement and is arguably the most sophisticated software development organization in the world. The SEL uses the following formula to estimate effort on its projects:

$$Effort = 1.27 * KSLOC^{0.986}$$

In spite of its small type, the exponent of 0.986 points to a momentous difference between the SEL's formula and the formulas used by every other software organization in existence. Every other published estimation model uses an exponent greater than 1.0. The fact that the SEL's exponent is less than 1.0 suggests that the SEL is achieving a slight *economy* of scale. The process improvement carrot this represents is that sufficiently mature organizations might be able to turn the large-project problem on its head. They might actually be able to improve per-person productivity slightly as their projects become larger. This is a logical consequence of the specialization I discuss in Chapter 11.

If you consider the level of effectiveness available to organizations that operate at a high level of process sophistication, it becomes clear that the Ptolemaic practices are actually the old practices like code-and-fix development. A focus on process allows organizations to become more productive, produce software with fewer defects, take on more risk, improve their estimates, raise morale, and do better on large projects. What's not to like?

Serious Commitment

One thing not to like is that organizational improvement isn't easy. James Herbsleb surveyed organizations that had performed SW-CMM improvement. Seventy-seven percent of respondents said that organizational improvement took longer than expected, and 68 percent said it cost more than expected. Succeeding at SW-CMM improvement depends on these factors:

◆ Commitment from top management, including providing leadership and funding, prioritizing long-term improvement as a high priority, and actively monitoring the progress of process improvement.

◆ Establishment of a Software Engineering Process Group (SEPG). More than one SEPG may be required in a large organization. The SEPG must be staffed with senior people who understand their roles as internal consultants, the organization's improvement goals, and the cultural issues involved in process improvement.

◆ Appropriate training for middle management and technical staff, along with performance rewards that are aligned with long-term SW-CMM objectives.

This is a highly simplified list, and each organization will have additional specialized factors that will affect its improvement initiative. As I mentioned in Chapter 2, some organizations implement SW-CMM as a buzzword du jour. Attempts to treat the SW-CMM as yet another silver bullet are not likely to succeed.

Organizational Ratings

The SW-CMM is a mature, effective model for organizational improvement. Because it stratifies software organizations into different levels of effectiveness, it is also an effective model for organizational assessment. Other, more mature professions use organizational assessment as part of their program for maintaining a high standard of practice. Accounting firms are required to go through a peer review every three years. Colleges are accredited for a maximum of three years and must be re-reviewed before their accreditation expires. Some individual programs within colleges are accredited separately from the college. Hospitals are accredited by the Joint Commission on Accreditation of Healthcare Organizations (JCAHO) and are accredited for a maximum of three years.

JCAHO lists these reasons that a hospital would seek accreditation:

◆   Enhances community confidence

◆   Provides a report card for the public

◆   Offers an objective evaluation of the organization's performance

◆   Stimulates the organization's quality improvement efforts

◆   Aids in professional staff recruitment

◆   Provides a staff education tool

◆   May be used to meet certain Medicare certification requirements

◆   Expedites third-party payment

◆   Often fulfills state licensure requirements

◆   May favorably influence liability insurance premiums

◆   Favorably influences managed care contract decisions

Accreditation is a voluntary process, but most hospitals try to maintain accreditation for the reasons listed.

The parallels to software organizational assessment are clear. SW-CMM assessments provide a report card that potential clients can use in evaluating software contracting arrangements or packaged software purchases. They provide an objective, publicly recognized standard of comparison. They stimulate quality improvement efforts by encouraging organizations to improve their level rankings. It's easy to imagine insurance companies providing better rates on errors and omissions policies to companies operating at higher maturity levels. And if software follows other engineering disciplines, level rankings may even be used to fulfill state licensure requirements for organizations.

Form and Substance

There's an old saying that goes:

*Success = Planning * Execution*

If you assign a number between 0.0 and 1.0 to planning and do the same for execution, you will get a value for success that ranges from 0.0 to 1.0. If either planning or execution is missing, your chance of success will be 0.0.

What is important about the SW-CMM is its substance, not its form. Organizations that focus on SW-CMM–style improvement solely for the sake of getting a Level 2 or 3 rating will likely have half-baked planning and half-hearted execution. They are unlikely to achieve the numeric designation they want or the quality and productivity benefits they should want. This approach truly is Ptolemaic reasoning—letting the substance revolve around the form instead of putting the substance at the center of the software solar system. Organizations that focus on the bottom-line quality and productivity benefits offered by SW-CMM–style improvements are likely to take their planning more seriously and execute better. Those organizations will likely achieve better productivity, better quality, and, if they want to make it official, the Level 2, 3, 4, or 5 they deserve.

8

Body of Knowledge

"Truth will come sooner out of error than from confusion."
—*Francis Bacon*

A person needs to know about 50,000 chunks of information to be an expert in a field, where a chunk is any piece of knowledge that can be remembered rather than derived. In mature fields, a world-class expert typically needs at least 10 years to acquire that much knowledge. Some people argue that software-related knowledge isn't stable enough to be codified into a well-defined body of knowledge. They say that half of what a person needs to know to develop software today will be obsolete within three years. If the half-life claim is true, in the 10 years an expert would need to learn 50,000 chunks of information, 30,000 of those chunks would become obsolete. Software engineers would be like Sisyphus, pushing a boulder up a mountain only to have the boulder roll down the mountain as soon as it reached the top.

What are the half-lives of Java, Perl, HTML, C++, Linux, and Microsoft Windows NT? All these technologies are highly relevant as I write this book, but will they still be relevant by the time you read it? The half-life claim might well be true for technology-related knowledge. But another kind of software development knowledge is likely to serve a professional programmer throughout his or her career, and that knowledge is not subject to these same limitations.

Essence and Accident

In 1987, Fred Brooks published an influential article, "No Silver Bullets—Essence and Accident in Software Engineering." Its main contention is that no single tool or methodology—no "silver bullet"—portended a 10-to-1 improvement in productivity over the next decade. The reasoning behind this claim helps in identifying software development knowledge not subject to the 3-year half-life.

In using the words "essence" and "accident," Brooks draws on an ancient philosophical tradition of distinguishing between "essential" and "accidental" properties. Essential properties are those properties that a thing must have to be that thing: a car must have an engine, wheels, and a transmission to be a car. A car might have a V8 or an in-line six, studded snow tires or racing slicks, an automatic transmission or a stick shift. These are accidental properties, the properties that arise by happenstance and that do not affect the basic "car-ness" of the car. The term "accidental" can be confusing, but it just means nonessential or optional.

According to Brooks, the most difficult work of software development is not in representing the concepts faithfully in a specific computer programming language (coding) or checking the fidelity of that representation (testing). Coding and testing are the accidental parts of software development. The essence of software development, Brooks argues, consists of working out the specification, design, and verification of a highly precise and richly detailed set of interlocking concepts. He says that software development is difficult because of its essential complexity, conformity, changeability, and invisibility.

Computer programs are *complex* by nature. Even if you could invent a programming language that operated exactly at the level of the problem domain, programming would be a complicated activity because you would need to precisely define relationships between real-world entities, identify exception cases, anticipate all possible state transitions, and so on. Strip away the accidental work involved in representing these factors in a specific programming language and in a specific computing environment, and you still have the essential difficulty of defining the underlying real-world concepts and debugging your understanding of them.

Another essential difficulty of software development arises from the need for software to *conform* to messy real-world constraints such as pre-existing hardware, third-party components, government regulations, business rules, and legacy data formats. The software designer often faces inflexible external considerations that limit the extent to which complexity can be reduced.

Software's *changeability* presents another essential difficulty for software development. The more successful a program is, the more uses people will find for it, and the more it will be adapted beyond the domain for which it was originally intended. As the software grows, it becomes more complex and must conform to additional constraints. The more software is adapted, the more involved the adaptations become.

A final essential difficulty arises from software's inherent *invisibility*. Software can't be visualized with 2-D or 3-D geometric models. Attempts to visually represent even simple logic quickly become absurdly complicated, as anyone who has ever tried to draw a flow chart for even a simple program will attest.

Brooks argues that software development has already made all possible major gains in the accidental elements. These gains include the invention of high-level languages, adoption of interactive computing, and development of powerful integrated environments. Any further order-of-magnitude productivity improvements, he says, can be made only by addressing software development's essential difficulties, described above.

Defining a Stable Core

Knowledge that helps developers deal with what Brooks calls the essential difficulties of software development is what I think of as *software engineering principles*, which are software engineering's core body of knowledge. In 1968, NATO held the first conference on software engineering. Using the term "software engineering" to describe the body of knowledge that existed at that time was premature, and it was intended to be provocative.

Exactly how small was the stable core of software engineering knowledge in 1968? Consider that the first fully correct binary search algorithm was published only six years before the NATO conference. C. Böhm and G. Jacopini published the paper that established the theoretical foundation for eliminating *goto* and the creation of structured programming only two years before the conference, in 1966. Edsger Dijkstra wrote his famous letter to the editor, "GoTo Statement Considered Harmful," in 1968. At the time the conference was held, subroutines were a fairly new idea, and programmers regularly debated whether the subroutines were really useful. Larry Constantine, Glenford Myers, and Wayne Stevens didn't publish the first paper on structured design until 1974. Tom Gilb published the first book on software metrics in 1977, and Tom DeMarco published the first book on software requirements analysis in 1979. People trying to identify a stable core of knowledge in 1968 would have had their work cut out for them.

Researchers at Université du Québec à Montréal have spearheaded an effort to identify the generally accepted elements of software engineering. Coordinated by the ACM and the IEEE Computer Society and involving both academic and industrial participants, this effort is called the Software Engineering Body of Knowledge project, or SWEBOK. From an analysis of the SWEBOK project's body of knowledge areas (which I'll discuss later in this chapter), I estimate that the half-life of software engineering's body of knowledge in 1968 was only about 10 years. As Figure 8-1 illustrates, the stable core was relatively small, and I estimate that only about 10–20 percent of software engineering knowledge from 1968 is still in use today.

Software engineering has made significant progress since 1968. Hundreds of thousands of pages have been written on the topic. Professional societies host hundreds of conferences and workshops every year. Knowledge has been codified into more than 2000 pages of IEEE software engineering standards. Dozens of universities across North America offer graduate education in software engineering, and a few around the world are beginning to offer undergraduate programs.

The absence of perfectly stable software engineering knowledge hardly makes the field unique. In the 1930s, the medical profession did not yet know about penicillin, the structure of DNA, or the genetic basis of many diseases, and it did not have technologies such as heart-lung machines and magnetic resonance imaging. And yet medicine was a recognized profession.

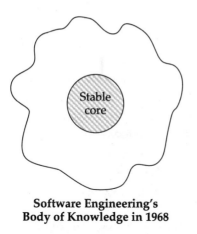

**Software Engineering's
Body of Knowledge in 1968**

FIGURE 8-1   *As of the 1968 NATO Conference on Software Engineering, only about 10–20 percent of the software engineering body of knowledge was stable (i.e., would still be relevant 30 years later). The half-life of the software engineering body of knowledge at that time was about 10 years.*

As Figure 8-2 suggests, based on my analysis OF SWEBOK'S knowledge areas, I estimate that the stable core now makes up about 50 percent of the knowledge needed to develop a software system. That increase might not seem like a dramatic change from the 10–20 percent of 1968, but it implies that the body of knowledge's half-life has improved from about 10 years to about 30 years. Today the educational investment a person makes at the beginning of a career in software will remain largely relevant throughout that person's career.

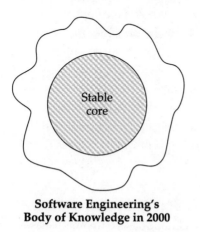

**Software Engineering's
Body of Knowledge in 2000**

FIGURE 8-2   *As of today, about 50 percent of the software engineering body of knowledge is stable and will still be relevant 30 years from now.*

Stabilization of software engineering's body of knowledge puts software engineering on an educational footing similar to that of other engineering disciplines. As Dave Parnas points out, the content of a physics class can remain unchanged even if the lab gets a new oscilloscope. Most of the content of software engineering courses can be independent of specific short-lived technologies such as C++ and Java. Students will have to learn those technologies in the lab, but in the classroom they can focus on more lasting knowledge.

Software Engineering's Body of Knowledge

In Chapter 4, I argued that software engineering is not the same as computer science, but if it isn't computer science, what is it? Those of us working in software development now have an exciting opportunity to watch a new field being born. For more established fields such as mathematics, physics, and psychology, we tend to take the contents of the field for granted, assuming that the definition of what is in and what is out of the field has always been the way it is and has to be that way. But at some point people working in each field developed textbooks and university curriculums that required them to decide what knowledge was in and what was out. For hundreds of years, people didn't differentiate between mathematics, physics, psychology, and philosophy. Physics began to be treated as separate from philosophy about 1600. Psychology wasn't distinguished from philosophy until about 1900.

In defining what knowledge is in and what is out of the field of software engineering, experts recommend that the focus be on generally accepted knowledge and practices. As Figure 8-3 suggests, "generally accepted" refers to the knowledge and practices that are applicable to most projects most of the time—practices that most experts would agree are valuable and useful. This definition does not imply that the established knowledge and practices should be applied uniformly to all projects. Project leaders should still be responsible for determining the most appropriate practices for any particular project.

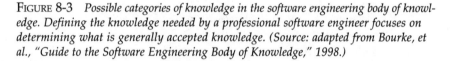

FIGURE 8-3   *Possible categories of knowledge in the software engineering body of knowledge. Defining the knowledge needed by a professional software engineer focuses on determining what is generally accepted knowledge. (Source: adapted from Bourke, et al., "Guide to the Software Engineering Body of Knowledge," 1998.)*

Since 1968, we've made significant progress in the areas Brooks referred to as the essential difficulties of software development. We now have adequate or good reference books on requirements engineering, design, construction, testing, reviews, quality assurance, software project management, algorithms, and user interface design, just to name a few topics. New and better books that codify software engineering knowledge are appearing regularly. Some core elements have not yet been brought together in practical textbooks or courses, and in that sense our body of knowledge is still fragmented and under construction. But the basic knowledge about how to perform each of these practices is available—in journal articles, conference papers, and seminars as well as in books. (These books are listed on the professionalism web site described at the back of the book.) The pioneers of software engineering have already blazed the trails and surveyed the land. Now the software engineering settlers need to build the roads and develop the rest of the education and accreditation infrastructure.

Figure 8-4 shows that software engineering draws from computer science, mathematics, cognitive sciences (psychology and sociology), project management, and various engineering disciplines.

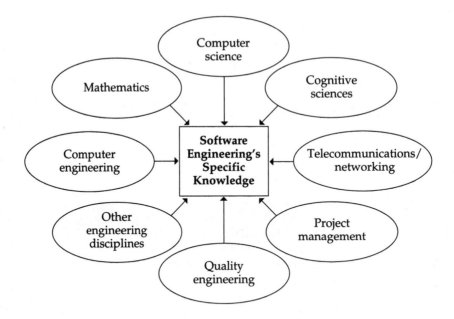

FIGURE 8-4 *Sources of knowledge in software engineering's body of knowledge. (Source: adapted from Tripp, "Professionalism of Software Engineering: Next Steps," 1999.)*

Using the knowledge areas in Figure 8-4 plus knowledge that has developed uniquely within software engineering, SWEBOK identified the following knowledge areas that make up the core competencies for a professional software engineer. The terminology is still being defined, so for each area listed here, I've used the term I think is clearest.

◆ *Software Requirements Engineering* The discovery, documentation, and analysis of the functions to be implemented in software.

◆ *Software Design* Definition of the basic structure of the system at the architectural and detailed levels, division into modules, definition of interfaces for modules, and choice of algorithms within modules.

◆ *Software Construction* Implementation of the software including detailed design, coding, debugging, unit testing, technical reviews, and performance optimization. This area overlaps somewhat with Software Design and Software Testing.

◆ *Software Testing*   All activities associated with executing software to detect defects and evaluate features. Testing includes test planning, test case design, and specific kinds of tests such as development tests, unit tests, component tests, integration tests, system tests, regression tests, stress tests, and acceptance tests.

◆ *Software Evolution and Maintenance*   Revision and enhancement of existing software, related documentation, and tests.

◆ *Software Configuration Management*   Identification, documentation, and change control of all intellectual property generated on a software project, including source code, content (graphics, sound, text, video), requirements, designs, test materials, estimates, plans, and user documentation.

◆ *Software Quality Engineering*   All activities associated with providing confidence that a software item conforms or will conform to technical requirements. Quality engineering includes quality assurance planning, quality measurement, reliability, testing, technical reviews, audits, and verification and validation.

◆ *Software Engineering Management*   Planning; tracking; and controlling of a software project, software work, or a software organization.

◆ *Software Engineering Infrastructure*   Tool and methodology support, such as CASE tools, reusable code libraries, and formal methods, including practices for adopting and disseminating tools and methods within an organization.

◆ *Software Engineering Process*   Activities related to improving software development quality, timeliness, productivity, and other project and product characteristics.

The extent of this list might surprise some people. Many practicing programmers work as though Software Construction is the only knowledge area that matters. As important as that area is, it is only one of 10 areas that a professional software engineer should know.

Other practicing programmers might be surprised at the complete absence of specific languages and programming environments—Java, C++, Linux, Microsoft Windows NT, and so on. That's because the body of knowledge emphasizes software engineering principles rather than knowledge of technology.

A few people's reactions to these knowledge areas will be, "That's a lot to expect someone to learn just to write computer programs." It is a lot to expect people to learn, and historically we've been expecting them to learn it implicitly, through on-the-job exposure to new information. The result is that most practicing computer programmers have pretty good knowledge of Software Construction and Software Evolution and Maintenance; marginal knowledge of Software Requirements, Software Design, Software Testing, and Software Engineering Infrastructure; and virtually no knowledge of Software Configuration Management, Software Quality Engineering, Software Management, or Software Engineering Process. Professional fields are characterized by in-depth education, and software engineering is no exception.

I don't expect software engineers to achieve mastery in each of these areas, but a professional software engineer should at least acquire introductory knowledge of all areas, competence in most, and mastery of some. As I described in Chapter 4, one of the differences between a scientist and an engineer is that scientists can afford to have knowledge that is narrow and deep whereas engineers need broad understanding of all the factors that affect the products they create.

First Vintage

Is this definition of software engineering's body of knowledge the final answer? No. The field of medicine has continued to evolve, and the field of software engineering will continue to evolve too. But there is great value in planting a stake in the ground and saying, "This is what constitutes the software engineering body of knowledge at this time."

As Francis Bacon pointed out when he laid the foundation for modern science almost 400 years ago, errors are a better basis for progress than confusion is. Bacon knew that when his systematic approach was used, many of the initial conclusions it produced—the "first vintages"—would be mistaken. But those mistakes would be used to direct further inquiry, and they were part of his plan. Major elements of our current definition of the software engineering body of knowledge will undoubtedly turn out to be mistaken, but an imperfect, clear definition will give us a baseline upon which we can improve. The approach used on the typical software project today is so incoherent that it's sometimes hard even to tell what practices are being used. Exchanging the current confused muddle for a clearly defined body of knowledge is a good trade, errors and all.

9

Novum Organum

---◆---

"A prudent question is one-half wisdom."
—Francis Bacon

---◆---

In 1620, Francis Bacon published the *Novum Organum,* a masterwork that challenged Bacon's contemporaries to discard their ancient reliance on pure deductive reasoning and embrace a scientific method based on observation and experience. He imagined a new world of culture and leisure that could be gained by inquiry into the laws and processes of nature. In describing this world, he anticipated the effects of advances in science, engineering, and technology. Bacon's scientific method consisted of three steps:

◆ Purge your mind of prejudices—what Bacon called "superstition."

◆ Collect observations and experiences systematically.

◆ Stop, survey what you have seen, and draw initial conclusions—
the "first vintage." Use these conclusions to direct further inquiry.

Novum Organum is part of a larger work called *Instauratio Magna*, which
sets out to organize the sciences, define a method of scientific inquiry, collect observations and facts, present examples of the new method, and define
a new philosophy based on the results of this scientific work. Bacon's writing
so influenced modern scientific methods that he is often called the Father of
Modern Science.

The title page of *Novum Organum*, shown in Figure 9-1, contains an image of a ship passing through the Pillars of Hercules. The Pillars of Hercules
were generally accepted to have stood on the sides of the Strait of Gibraltar,
the sole passage between the Mediterranean Sea and the Atlantic Ocean. For
the ancients, the Pillars of Hercules symbolized the limits of human's possible explorations. Beyond the pillars lay the edge of the earth; the ancients
had not been inclined to progress into those outer reaches and leave the old
world behind.

FIGURE 9-1 *The title page from Bacon's* Instauratio Magna, *which contains his*
Novum Organum. *The ancients were reluctant to sail beyond the Pillars of Hercules.*

Today, average software development practices are becalmed in a windless sea of code-and-fix programming—a kind of flat-earth approach to software development that was proven ineffective 20 years ago. Leading software engineers have a clear idea of what lies beyond software's Pillars of Hercules. Software engineering has already had its Marco Polo, Vasco da Gama, and Ferdinand Magellan. As Chapter 7 describes, vast software riches await in waters that have been charted extensively but that are traveled infrequently by average software practitioners.

The Profession Defined

Considering the disparity between the best software organizations and the worst, the current challenge is not so much to advance the state of the art as it is to raise the average level of practice. The new world has been adequately explored; it's time to start colonizing. The traditional means of raising the level of practice in a field, especially one that affects the public welfare, is through establishment of a formal profession.

Although the term is often used casually, the notion of a "profession" has a long and well-defined legal standing. The Code of Federal Regulations (CFR) in the United States says that a person employed in a "professional capacity" can be distinguished by several characteristics. A professional's work typically requires advanced knowledge in science or a field of learning that is acquired through a prolonged course of specialized study. The CFR distinguishes this advanced knowledge from a general academic education. It also distinguishes it from training in routine processes, whether they be mental, manual, or physical. The CFR goes on to note that professional work can be creative and artistic. The work may depend primarily on the inventiveness, imagination, or talent of the person doing the work.

The CFR also states that professional work requires the consistent exercise of discretion and judgment in its performance and that it is predominantly intellectual and varied in character. The CFR again differentiates this from routine mental, manual, mechanical, or physical work.

Most software developers will recognize characteristics of their own work in the CFR's description of a profession. The work certainly requires advanced knowledge (detailed technical knowledge, anyway), and it benefits from specialized instruction and study. Software development contains a significant creative element and clearly calls for a great deal of discretion and judgment. In short, the work performed by software developers seems to meet the definition of "professional work" as defined in the CFR.

The CFR contributes part of the legal definition of a profession. The body of legal precedents (court cases) establishes a slightly different but complementary definition. According to legal precedents, a profession has the following attributes:

◆   A requirement for extensive learning and training

◆   A code of ethics imposing standards higher than those normally tolerated in the marketplace

◆   A disciplinary system for professionals who breach the code

◆   A primary emphasis on social responsibility over strictly individual gain, and a corresponding duty of its members to behave as members of a disciplined and honorable profession

◆   A prerequisite of a license prior to admission to practice

How well does software engineering rate according to these criteria?

In Search of a Software Engineering Profession

Gary Ford and Norman E. Gibbs of the Software Engineering Institute identified eight elements of a mature profession, which follow. A professional's development typically follows the progression shown in Figure 9-2.

Initial Professional Education   Professionals generally begin their professional lives by completing a university program in their chosen fields—law school, medical school, engineering school, and so on.

Accreditation   University programs are accredited by oversight bodies that determine whether the programs provide adequate education. Accreditation assures that graduates from accredited programs start their professional lives with the knowledge they need to perform effectively. The Accreditation Board for Engineering and Technology (ABET) oversees engineering programs.

Skills Development   For most professions, education alone is not sufficient to develop full professional capabilities. Nascent professionals need practice applying their knowledge before they are prepared to take primary responsibility for performing work in their fields. Physicians have a three-year residency. Certified public accountants (CPAs) must work one year for a board-approved organization before receiving their licenses. Professional engineers must have at least four years of work experience. Requiring some kind of apprenticeship assures that people who enter a profession have practice performing work at a satisfactory level of competence.

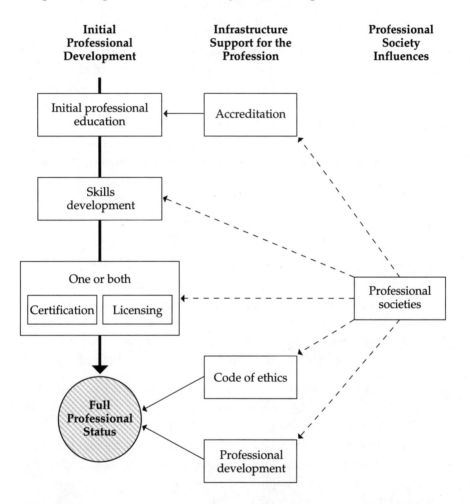

FIGURE 9-2   *Professional development follows most or all of these basic steps in all well-established professions.*

Certification   After completion of education and skills development, a professional is required to pass one or more exams that assure the person has attained a minimum level of knowledge. Doctors take board exams. Accountants take CPA exams. Professional engineers take a Fundamentals of Engineering exam at college graduation time and then take an engineering specialty exam about four years later. Some professions require recertification from time to time.

Licensing   Licensing is similar to certification except that it is mandatory instead of voluntary and is administered by a governmental authority.

Professional Development   Many professionals are required to keep their professional education current. Ongoing professional education maintains or improves workers' knowledge and skills after they begin professional practice. Professional development requirements tend to be strongest in professions where a body of technical knowledge is rapidly changing. Medicine is perhaps the most notable because of the constant improvements in drugs, therapies, medical equipment, and diagnosis and treatment procedures. After a professional's initial education and skills development are complete, this additional education requirement helps to assure a minimum competency level throughout the professional's career.

Professional Societies   Professionals see themselves as part of a community of like-minded individuals who put their professional standards above their individual self-interest or their employer's self-interest. When a professional society is just beginning, it usually promotes the exchange of knowledge, and over time its function evolves to include defining certification criteria, managing certification programs, establishing accreditation standards, and defining a code of ethics and disciplinary action for violations of that code.

Code of Ethics   Each profession has a code of ethics to ensure that its practitioners behave responsibly. The code states not just what its practitioners actually do but what they should do. Professionals can be ejected from their professional societies or lose their licenses to practice for violating the code of ethics. Adherence to a recognized code of conduct helps professionals feel they belong to a well-regarded community, and enforcement of ethics standards helps maintain a minimum level of conduct.

In addition to the eight elements identified by Ford and Gibbs, many professions exhibit a ninth characteristic that applies to organizations rather than specific workers:

Organizational Certification   In many professions, not only must individuals be certified, their organizations must be certified. Accounting firms are peer reviewed. Hospitals are accredited, as are universities. For fields as complex as accounting, education, and medicine, organizational certification is a response to the reality that individual competence is not sufficient to guarantee adequate levels of professional service; organizational characteristics can have as much influence as individuals' characteristics.

Ford and Gibbs point out that many nonprofessional occupations exhibit some small number of these elements. For example, the state of California requires licenses for custom upholsterers, amateur boxers, private investigators, and mule racing jockeys, but it doesn't require most of the other elements of a profession for those occupations. For many professions, nearly all of the elements exist.

Ford and Gibbs defined several levels of maturity for each of the elements of a profession:

◆   *Nonexistence*   The element simply doesn't exist.

◆   *Ad Hoc*   The element exists but only in isolated, uncoordinated instances.

◆   *Established*   The element exists and is clearly identified with a profession. (Ford and Gibbs use the word "specific," but I use "established" because I think it is clearer.)

◆   *Maturing*   The element has existed for many years and is actively maintained and improved by some professional body.

A mature profession is one whose elements have reached the Maturing stage. Of course, "maturity" is a moving target. Some of the specific elements that seemed mature 30 years ago don't seem mature today, and others that seem mature today will not seem mature 30 years from now.

Table 9-1 describes the maturity of the software engineering profession. The profession is mostly in the Established stage, with some areas lagging and some moving into the Maturing stage. More details about the entries in the table are discussed throughout this book.

TABLE 9-1 MATURITY OF THE SOFTWARE ENGINEERING PROFESSION

Element	Current Status
Initial Professional Education	Ad Hoc, moving toward Established. Bachelor's degrees in computer science, electrical engineering, mathematics, and so on are the typical preparation for entry into the profession. Several master's degree programs in software engineering exist. A few undergraduate programs are underway to produce software engineering graduates.
Accreditation	Ad Hoc. Accreditation guidelines are currently being defined by a joint working group from the ACM and IEEE Computer Society but have not yet been implemented.
Skills Development	Established. Guidelines have been developed for the skills needed by a software engineer to enter the profession.
Certification	Ad Hoc, moving toward Established. Commercial vendors such as Microsoft, Novell, and Oracle provide technology-related certification programs. No universally recognized professional certification standard exists.
Licensing	Ad Hoc, moving toward Established. The state of Texas licenses professional software engineers under a statute passed in 1998. The province of British Columbia began registering professional software engineers in 1999.
Professional Development	Ad Hoc, moving toward Established. Some organizations have published professional development guidelines. For one example, see Construx Software's guidelines at www.construx.com/profession/.
Professional Societies	Established, moving toward Maturing. The ACM, the IEEE Computer Society, and other professional societies exist. These societies (especially the IEEE) explicitly state that they represent software engineering. They do not yet offer the full range of products and services needed to support software engineers as professionals. They do not manage a certification program and cannot discipline violators of the software engineering code of ethics.
Code of Ethics	Established. The ACM and the IEEE Computer Society have adopted a code of ethics specifically for software engineers. The code is not yet widely respected or adopted within industry.
Organizational Certification	Established, moving toward Maturing. The Software Engineering Institute has defined a Software Capability Maturity Model that it actively maintains and improves. The model has been used to assess more than 1000 organizations since 1987. It is not applied universally. ISO 9000-9004 certification is widely adopted, especially in Europe.

Through the Pillars

Software engineering does not fully meet the definition of a "profession" at this time. Initial education is hit or miss. Licensing is available to only a tiny fraction of current software workers. A code of ethics exists, but it isn't enforced. Much work is being done, however, to accelerate the movement of software engineering into the Established and Maturing stages.

Software developers work in a technical field, but many aren't very technical when choosing software practices. They cling emotionally to code-and-fix development rather than choosing practices based on analytical assessments of what works best. If we apply Bacon's scientific method to software engineering, we can see the three steps we must take to "get technical" about software engineering:

Purge your mind of prejudices   The software industry needs to kick its addiction to code-and-fix development, a prejudice that has a long track record of benefiting no one.

Collect observations and experiences systematically   A few organizations have begun collecting data on the effectiveness of their development practices and evaluating which practices make them most successful. Some have achieved dramatic results. Other organizations need to follow.

Stop, survey what you have seen, and draw initial conclusions   This book presents the initial conclusions. Software development is at a major decision point. We can stay safe in our code-and-fix harbor, not venturing past the pillars of Hercules and not achieving the significant gains that have already been discovered by software engineering explorers. Or we can boldly venture toward a true profession of software engineering. I, for one, plan to leave the old world behind and begin colonizing a new world of higher productivity, lower costs, shorter schedules, and higher quality.

III

THROUGH THE PILLARS

10 *Stinking Badges*

---◆---

"Badges? We ain't got no badges. We don't need no badges.
I don't have to show you any stinking badges."
—*Gold Hat Bandito*, Treasure of the Sierra Madre

---◆---

F ew issues are as controversial to software developers as licensing and certification, and in few areas are the conclusions as inescapable. If you are a software developer who plans to be in the field for 10 years or more, you will have to confront these issues.

Certification

Certification is a voluntary process administered by a professional society. The intent of certification is to give the public a way of knowing who is qualified to perform specific kinds of work. Certification requirements usually include both education and experience. In most cases, a written examination is used to determine the competency of the individual seeking certification. Certification usually extends beyond a limited geographic area to national or international regions. The best-known example of professional certification in the United States is that of the certified public accountant.

Some organizations have offered certification for software workers for many years. The Institute for Certification of Computing Professionals offers Associate Computing Professional and Certified Computing Professional designations. The American Society for Quality Control offers a Software Quality Engineer designation (although the organization's usage of the term "engineer" may expose it to legal problems because the term is regulated by most states and throughout Canada). At this time, there is no universally accepted certification program for software engineers.

Many companies offer certification programs related to specific technologies. Microsoft offers a Microsoft Certified Professional designation. Novell offers a Certified Network Engineer designation, Oracle offers an Oracle Certified Professional designation, and Apple Computer offers the Apple Certified Server Engineer designation. The focus of this kind of certification is limited to a single company's products, which makes it narrower than true software engineering certification would be.

Software is mysterious and complex enough that nonsoftware practitioners need help in selecting qualified technical personnel. Certification offers employers and customers a way to recognize software personnel who have achieved at least some minimum level of qualification. The market is already supporting this—at the time I write this book, Amazon.com lists 25 categories of books on various kinds of software-related and computer-related certification exams. Nearly all these exams are related to specific technologies. A widely recognized, broader software engineering certification program would be a useful addition to the field.

Licensing

Licensing is a mandatory, legal process that is intended to protect the public, and it is typically administered by jurisdictions (states, provinces, and territories). For many professions, national organizations advise the jurisdictions on appropriate licensing requirements and exam contents.

Most professions are licensed, including the professions of doctor, architect, lawyer, and engineer. No occupation that affects the public as much as software does remains unlicensed. The following list gives examples of occupations that require licenses in the state of California.

- Acupuncturist
- Alarm company operator
- Amateur boxer
- Architect
- Attorney
- Barber
- Certified public accountant
- Contractor
- Cosmetologist
- Custom upholsterer
- Dentist
- Embalmer
- Family counselor
- Funeral director
- Geologist
- Guide dog instructor
- Hearing aid dispenser
- Jockey
- Locksmith
- Manicurist
- Mule jockey
- Nurse
- Pest control operator
- Physician
- Physician's assistant
- Private investigator
- Professional engineer
- Real estate appraiser
- Repossessor
- Retail furniture dealer
- Veterinarian

In engineering the majority of engineers do not obtain licenses. Engineering companies are required to employ some licensed engineers, but not all of their engineers have to be licensed. Almost half of civil engineers are licensed, whereas only 8 percent of chemical engineers are licensed. The difference lies in how replicable the engineered artifact is and how much impact the item has on public safety. Artifacts that are replicated in large numbers can be tested before they are manufactured and sold to the public; this testing generally minimizes the risk to the public and reduces the number of licensed engineers needed for a particular kind of work.

Civil engineers design many one-of-a-kind, safety-critical artifacts—highways, bridges, baseball stadiums, airport runways, and so on. Electrical engineers design artifacts that are reproduced in large quantities—toasters, televisions, telephones, and so on. So, as Table 10-1 shows, more civil engineers than electrical engineers are licensed.

PERCENTAGE OF LICENSED
TABLE 10-1   ENGINEERING GRADUATES IN THE U.S. AS OF 1996

Discipline	Licensed
Civil	44%
Mechanical	23%
Electrical	9%
Chemical	8%
All engineers	18%

Where would software engineers fit into this table? We produce many one-of-a-kind artifacts, but we also produce operating systems, tax preparation software, word processors, and other programs that are replicated by the millions. We produce some safety-critical systems, but we produce many more business systems that have less significant impacts on the public safety. On balance, perhaps 5–10 percent of people currently practicing as computer programmers will eventually get their badges—their professional engineer licenses in software.

Bootstrap Licensing

The movement to license software developers began to gain momentum in 1998 when the Texas Board of Professional Engineers adopted software engineering as a distinct licensable engineering discipline, resulting in a professional engineer, or PE, designation for professional engineers specializing in software. The ACM and IEEE Computer Society are currently working with the Texas Board of Professional Engineers to create a Principles of Practice

Examination that will allow software professional engineers to obtain their licenses the same way other professional engineers do.

In the meantime, Texas has begun licensing professional software engineers under a restrictive exam-waiver clause. To obtain a PE license before the exam becomes available, an applicant must have *one* of the following:

◆   16 years of engineering experience

◆   12 years of engineering experience and a bachelor's degree from an accredited university program

◆   6 years of experience and a PhD in engineering or a related subject from a university whose undergraduate program is accredited

In addition, each applicant must provide at least nine references, at least five of which must be from licensed professional engineers (not necessarily software engineers). The same criteria for waiving the professional engineering exam apply to other engineering disciplines in Texas.

How many practicing software developers could qualify as professional software engineers under Texas's current licensing procedure? Not very many, and that's one of the smartest things the state of Texas has done. The natural tendency would be to make the exam-waiver clause so loose during the bootstrapping phase that most current practitioners would automatically qualify. The net effect of that would be to degrade the term "professional software engineer" to mean the same as "run-of-the-mill programmer." By making its exam-waiver clause restrictive, Texas has maximized the likelihood that professional software engineers will represent some of the best software developers in Texas, and it has safeguarded the reputation of the "professional software engineer" title.

Texas is significant because, along with New York and California, it is a bellwether state. Take the approval of high school textbooks, for example. Texas's approval clears the way for about 40 other states to approve a textbook automatically. Other states are watching Texas's software licensing actions carefully. Where Texas goes, others will follow.

After I wrote the first draft of this chapter and while I was awaiting comments from peer reviewers, the Association of Professional Engineers and Geoscientists of British Columbia (APEGBC) began registering software professional engineers (PEng) in British Columbia. Like Texas's program, APEGBC's program contains a bootstrapping provision that allows software developers with the appropriate combination of education and experience to obtain their professional engineering licenses.

Your Stake

One of the consequences of being a professional engineer is that you can be held personally liable for the work your company performs under your signature. Courts in the United States have held that only members of a profession can be found guilty of malpractice. Doctors, lawyers, and architects can be guilty of malpractice. Garbage truck drivers, short order cooks, and computer programmers cannot be guilty of malpractice because, legally, they aren't considered to be professionals. By establishing software engineering as a profession, we are paving the way for the courts to find software engineers liable for malpractice, just like other professionals. On the other hand, following commonly accepted engineering practices can be a defense in some cases.

Many programmers will choose not to become professional engineers. Some won't be interested in the studying required to pass the PE exam. Some will think that, since a PE designation doesn't guarantee an increase in salary, the reward doesn't justify the effort. Others will choose to avoid the possibility of personal liability.

The disadvantages of becoming a professional engineer might appear to outweigh the benefits, but inducements will come from both the government and software organizations. No individual engineer will be required to be licensed, but some companies will be. The kinds of companies that will be licensed is an open question and will depend on the political climate during the next few years and on the extent to which software-related problems catch the public's attention. The companies most likely to be required to employ professional engineers include:

- Companies that sell software engineering services to the public
- Companies that perform software work for public agencies
- Companies that produce safety-critical software

Other companies might voluntarily employ professional engineers to take advantage of the marketing cachet of hiring workers with the best available credentials or because they see hiring professional engineers as a way to strengthen their technical talent pool. (Hiring software engineers who have obtained certification but not professional engineering status might also serve these companies' interests.)

Professional engineers in these companies will review software engineering work and sign off on the software their companies deliver. To those companies, employing professional engineers will be a legal necessity, and, in the early days of licensing when professional engineers are in short supply, software companies will reward professional engineers accordingly. If software companies follow other engineering disciplines, the company that hires a professional engineer will pay for the professional engineer's liability insurance as part of the employment package, which will minimize that disadvantage of getting a professional engineering license.

Professional engineers will gain other benefits. The professional engineers who put their signatures and reputations on the line for their companies will have final say over methodology choices, design approaches, and other decisions that affect the quality of the software for which they might be held liable. Without professional standing, your boss can come to you and demand that you commit to an unrealistic schedule, make short-sighted design compromises, or sacrifice quality to get the software out the door. As Fred Brooks pointed out a quarter century ago, it's difficult to make a vigorous, job-risking defense of something that has no quantitative foundation and is certified chiefly by your hunches. A well-defined profession—consisting of education, a code of ethics, and licensing—will give you a stronger foundation than mere hunches. You will be able to say, "The standards of my profession don't allow me to shortchange quality in this situation. I could lose my license." You will have a professional and legal basis for standing up to unenlightened managers, marketers, and customers—a basis that is sorely lacking today.

People who choose not to become professional engineers will encounter a glass ceiling that prevents them from rising to the top of the technical ranks in companies that employ professional engineers. Above a certain technical level, companies will be disinclined to promote software developers who can't sign off on a software release. Achievement of professional engineering status also says a person is serious about his or her profession. That demonstrated commitment to the software field may improve promotion prospects too.

At the organizational level, we might see an interplay between an organization's SW-CMM rating (discussed in Chapter 7) and the professional engineering license. Professional engineers will potentially be liable for the software written under their supervision. Professional engineers won't be able to personally review every line of code on large projects. Even if the organization pays for professional engineers' liability policies, I think that professional engineers will generally want to work for organizations in which they receive the most technical and process support—in other words, organizations that have the most sophisticated software organizational infrastructure. I predict that we'll see a concentration of professional engineers in organizations that have achieved higher SW-CMM levels, reinforcing the phenomenon that Harlan Mills observed 20 years ago: good developers tend to cluster in effective organizations and bad developers in ineffective organizations.

Making Deputies

A key step in any mature licensing plan is a competency exam administered by each jurisdiction. The exam is carefully designed to cover the knowledge that every professional engineer should have. One purpose of the exam is to weed out workers who aren't skilled enough to be licensed, and another is to define knowledge areas that every worker who is licensed will know.

The form of the software professional engineer exam has not yet been determined, and this is another reason that all eyes are on Texas. Models from other professions vary. Certified public accountants take a four-part exam that is administered over two days plus a three-hour ethics exam. Lawyers take a three-day exam, including a half-day ethics exam. Professional engineers generally take an eight-hour exam that includes solving eight problems—four are answered in essay format and four require about 10 multiple-choice answers each. The specifics of exams in all these professions vary from one jurisdiction to another.

Canada's approach to licensing engineers is more examination-intensive than the United States's. In British Columbia, the current draft exam standard for a software engineering license requires three-hour exams on each of 10 topics, seven of which are mandatory and three of which are chosen from a set of optional topics. Here are the mandatory topics:

- Data structures
- Design and analysis of algorithms
- Digital computer architecture
- File and database systems
- Object-oriented analysis, design, and programming
- Operating systems
- Software design

Here are the optional exam topics from which applicants must choose three:

- Advanced object-oriented analysis and design
- Analysis and design of user interfaces
- Artificial intelligence and expert systems
- Computer communications networks
- Computer graphics
- Distributed systems
- Foundations of modeling and simulation
- Image processing
- Introduction to compilers
- Microprocessor-based systems
- Parallel computing
- Real-time systems
- Security in computing
- Software development for large-scale systems
- Software evolution and reengineering
- Software project management
- Software quality engineering

Exams by themselves aren't foolproof, and merely passing the software professional engineer exam will not be sufficient to obtain a license. A professional engineering license traditionally requires both work experience and a degree from an accredited engineering school. In software engineering the degree is problematic, because only one university in the United States currently offers an undergraduate degree in software engineering (Rochester Institute of Technology), and its program will not be accredited until 2001 at the earliest. We can expect a nondegree bootstrap-licensing phase to last 10–15 years until the university infrastructure is in place to graduate sufficient numbers of software engineers. For the same reason, I expect it will be at least another 10–15 years before we begin to see widespread legal requirements for professional engineering in software.

No Guarantees

One argument against licensing goes like this: "I worked with a guy who had a PhD, and he was a terrible programmer. His code was bad, and he was really slow. Another guy I worked with didn't even have a high school diploma, and he was the best programmer I've ever seen. Exams don't differentiate between good and bad programmers. Intelligence and aptitude are what make the difference. Programming is more art than science."

As I argued in Chapter 4, a computer science education is the most common kind of software development education. Software engineering is not computer science, and it's not surprising that someone with a PhD in computer science isn't necessarily a good programmer. The software engineering field has become deep enough over the past 30 years that mere intelligence is no longer sufficient, just as it has long been insufficient for the practice of medicine, accounting, law, and other professions.

Nonetheless, the argument that some less-qualified people might obtain licenses and some more-qualified people might be denied licenses contains a grain of truth. Licensing acts as a filter that improves the quality of the labor pool, but it is not perfect—just better than the alternatives. Figure 10-1 shows what the labor pool without professional licensing looks like.

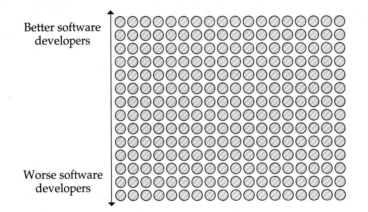

Better software
developers

Worse software
developers

FIGURE 10-1   *Pool of all software developers before the filter of professional licensing is applied.*

Without professional licensing, the public is exposed to both good and bad software development practices and is unprotected against potentially dangerous software. To protect the public interest, we would like the licensing procedure to act as a filter that denies licenses to the worst software developers and grants licenses to the best, as shown in Figure 10-2.

Realistically, licensing will not be an ideal filter. We all know good and bad attorneys, good and bad doctors, and good and bad practitioners from other professions. Even with the combination of exams, university education, and experience, the software-licensing filter won't be any better than filters for existing professions. Initially, the filter is likely to be worse because other professions have had more time to fine-tune their licensing exams and other requirements. As Figure 10-3 illustrates, even with the best current approaches, software licensing will allow a few unqualified people into the field and exclude a few who should have been licensed.

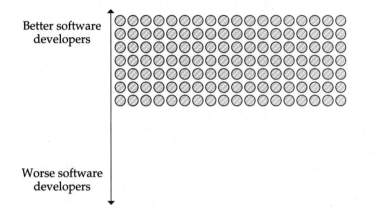

FIGURE 10-2   *Pool of software developers after professional licensing has been applied— assuming ideal licensing.*

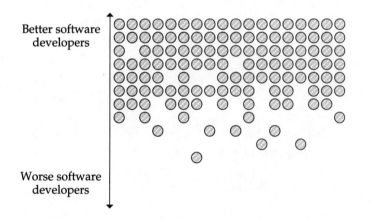

FIGURE 10-3   *Pool of software developers after professional licensing has been applied— assuming realistic licensing.*

The fact that ideal licensing isn't possible in no way implies that realistic licensing isn't valuable. Most software consumers would rather choose their software developers from the pool in Figure 10-3 than from the pool in Figure 10-1. The fact that some people might receive licenses or be denied licenses unfairly is not a compelling argument against licensing—today the general public sometimes receives excellent software, sometimes poor software, and sometimes software that puts their welfare at risk, and that's not fair either. And software developers who are unable to obtain their licenses—perhaps unfairly—will still be allowed to create software. They just won't be able to take primary responsibility for the most critical programs.

Stinking Badges or an Iron Ring?

In Canada, engineers who graduate from an accredited engineering program receive an iron ring at graduation time. Since 1923, the ring has been awarded in a secret ceremony that was developed by Rudyard Kipling. Tradition holds that these rings are made from the iron of a bridge that collapsed, and they symbolize each engineer's responsibility to society. Attempts have been made to bring the tradition of the iron ring to engineering graduates in the United States, but so far the practice is not widespread.

The iron ring is significant because, even though it doesn't designate full professional status, it does symbolize a commitment to engineering as a career. Certification may play a similar role in software—symbolizing a commitment to high standards of software engineering.

If you think, "We don't need no stinking badges or iron ring" you're right. The majority of software developers will choose not to attain their professional engineering licenses—their badges—even after licensing becomes widespread. The majority probably won't even bother with certification. But as the software engineering field matures, both licensing and certification will become more prominent. Developers who want to demonstrate a commitment to software engineering as a profession will get their licenses, certification, or both. If you want to run with the best, you'll need the metal.

11
Architects and Carpenters

---◆---

"Engineers produce plans. Builders implement the plans to produce a product."
—Terri Maginnis

---◆---

Within mature fields, occupations are both stratified and specialized. In the construction industry, architects and engineers produce the plans that general contractors build. General contractors typically subcontract parts of a job to specialty contractors such as framers, plumbers, and landscapers. The software industry is developing its own stratification into software architects and carpenters. It's also developing its own specialization into software framers, plumbers, and landscapers.

Software Engineering or Software *Engineering*?

Before we can discuss stratification or specialization, we need to define more precisely what a general "software engineer" is. Two defining uses of the term have emerged.

The first defining use of "software engineer" comes from David Parnas at McMaster University in Ontario, Canada. In Parnas's view, a software engineer is an engineer who has received special training in software development. Parnas contends that, to achieve full professional credentials and respect from other engineers, professional software engineers need to have the same educational foundation as other engineers. Moreover, software engineers often work in nuclear power plants, avionics software, manufacturing control, and other engineering areas in which knowledge of engineering fundamentals is beneficial or necessary. Students learning this kind of software engineering will take university courses in general chemistry, engineering mathematics, structure and properties of engineering materials, thermodynamics and heat transfer, and other courses that are traditionally part of an engineer's core education. They will also take courses that are part of a traditional computer science degree program.

The second defining use of "software engineer" comes from a program at Rochester Institute of Technology (RIT), which has been working with the ACM and IEEE Computer Society to develop a software engineering program that can be accredited by the Accreditation Board for Engineering and Technology (ABET). In this program, a software engineer is trained and educated to use an engineering approach to develop computer software. This kind of software engineer will take university courses in mathematics, software architecture, software requirements, programming of scientific applications, human factors, and other courses that sound more like computer science and management than traditional engineering. RIT currently offers a Software Engineering bachelor's degree designed along these lines. Table 11-1 summarizes the programs of study at McMaster University and RIT.

TABLE 11-1 COURSE REQUIREMENTS FOR SOFTWARE ENGINEERING PROGRAMS

Course	McMaster U. (Parnas)	RIT
Math and Science Chemistry, calculus, matrices, complex numbers, differential equations, discrete mathematics, probability and statistics	X	X
Introductory Engineering Structure and properties of engineering materials; dynamics and control of physical systems; thermodynamics and heat transfer; waves, electricity and magnetic fields	X	
Computer Science Introductory programming; digital system principles; computer architecture; logic design; data structures and algorithms; machine-level programming; programming language concepts; optimization methods, graph models, search and pruning techniques	X	X
Software Engineering Software architecture and design, requirements specification, professional communication skills, designing concurrent and real-time software, designing parallel and distributed systems, computation methods for science and engineering, user interface design	X	X
Software Engineering Management Software process and product metrics		X
Management Information Systems Principles of information systems design		X

Both of these programs are still under development, and of course two isolated university programs do not by themselves make a profession of software engineering. These specific programs will continue to evolve, and organizations including the IEEE Computer Society, ACM, ABET, local universities, and local licensing jurisdictions will influence the eventual development of the software engineering profession.

The subtle differences between these two programs point to an important difference in philosophy about software engineering. Parnas sees software engineers as engineers who develop software. The RIT program sees software engineers as programmers who use an engineering approach to develop software. These two views imply distinct software engineering curriculums and different relationships to existing engineering disciplines— and possibly distinct licensing and certification standards and examination procedures.

Programs like the McMaster University program will produce software engineers who can pass a Fundamentals of Engineering exam (also called the Engineer in Training exam in some areas) that all professional engineers in the United States and Canada must pass to eventually attain a professional engineer license (a PE in the United States or a PEng in Canada). RIT has defined a kind of software engineering that focuses more on software than on engineering. Programs like the RIT program won't provide software engineers with the engineering background needed to pass a Fundamentals of Engineering exam.

The differences between these two kinds of software engineering suggest that licensing will eventually progress along one of two roads. One road would lead to two kinds of professional credentials in software, the first being a traditional professional engineer with a specialty in software (PE or PEng). Individuals pursuing this credential would be educated in programs like the one at McMaster University and would follow the same career path that other engineers follow. The other professional credential would be more software-specific—Professional Software Engineer (PSE) or some such label—and would not require education in thermodynamics and heat transfer, structure and properties of engineering materials, and other traditional engineering topics. An argument in favor of this credential is that people designing business systems, financial applications, educational programs, and other software not used for engineering purposes really don't need knowledge of traditional engineering topics.

The second road would lead to modification of the Fundamentals of Engineering exams (the specific exams vary by jurisdiction) and creation of a specialty exam in software within the current engineering licensing framework. Most engineers today use computers extensively, and many create computer programs for their own use or for use by their colleagues. These programs provide data used in the design of bridges, skyscrapers, oil refineries, and many other structures that potentially impact the public welfare. The engineers writing these programs should have knowledge of effective software engineering practices. The Fundamentals of Engineering exams might simply need to be revised to contain more questions about software engineering. The exams are designed to be broad, and the score required to pass is fairly low—usually around 70 percent, although that varies by jurisdiction. Engineers trained in other disciplines will get more software answers wrong and traditional engineering answers right; software engineers will get more software answers right and traditional engineering answers wrong.

I think this second possibility is the better approach. Software engineers should take enough traditional engineering courses to understand how engineers in various disciplines think about design and problem solving. But they don't need to take every traditional engineering course to accomplish that. Software engineers could take fewer classes than are needed to pass current Fundamentals of Engineering exams and still pass a revised Fundamentals of Engineering exam.

Changes in the Fundamentals of Engineering exams wouldn't affect the caliber of engineers who are eventually granted licenses. Those engineers would still have to pass their engineering specialty exams at the end of their engineer-in-training period. Engineers' codes of ethics would still require them to practice only in fields within their areas of expertise. Introducing all engineers to software engineering knowledge might actually cause them to more fully appreciate the challenges associated with creating large computer systems, and they might be more willing to bring in expert help earlier when they work on projects that are beyond the scope of their education and training.

Stratification

The movement to license software developers and the debate over *software* engineers vs. software *engineers* are two signs that the software development field is becoming stratified just as other, more mature fields are. What will happen to the computer programmers who decide not to become professional engineers?

Many software developers will continue to work on projects that don't require them to obtain their professional engineering licenses. Many will work on projects that require someone to have a professional engineering license, but not them. And many will obtain other kinds of certification. Professional engineers in other disciplines are supported by engineering technicians and technologists. The National Institute for Certification in Engineering Technologies offers five kinds of certification for them. We see the same kind of stratification in medicine with doctors, physician's assistants, registered nurses, licensed practical nurses, and nurse's aides. In law, we see attorneys, paralegals, and legal secretaries. Complex fields become stratified.

As Figure 11-1 illustrates, as software licensing matures, software occupations will stratify into jobs that require more education and training and those that require less. Those that require more will command more responsibility, higher salaries, and greater prestige. The salaries claim might seem speculative, but I think it's a safe prediction because the general relationship between education and salary is so strong. In the United States, the average person who obtains a professional degree earns at least 50 percent more than the average person who obtains only a bachelor's degree. The average man who obtains a master's degree earns 20 percent more than the average man who obtains only a bachelor's degree. The average woman who obtains a master's degree earns 37 percent more than the average woman who obtains only a bachelor's degree. The Bureau of Labor Statistics reports that during the next five years demand will increase 5 percent for occupations requiring moderate on-the-job training and as much as 29 percent for occupations requiring a master's degree.

Some carpenters gripe about architects not knowing how to design a house properly, and some experienced carpenters do know more about the ins and outs of putting a house together than some architects. Basic programming skills can be taught at the tradesman level and don't require full-fledged software engineering education, training, or licensing. Some experienced coders will know more about the detailed aspects of making software work than some newly minted professional software engineers. But the people who put their names on the blueprints will have a different set of occupational rights and responsibilities than the carpenters have, regardless of who has more practical experience.

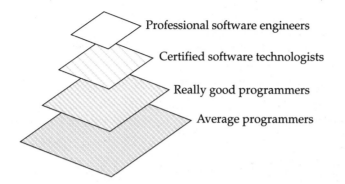

Professional software engineers

Certified software technologists

Really good programmers

Average programmers

FIGURE 11-1   *The software development field is stratifying into different levels of professional standing. The most highly trained software workers will generally command the most responsibility and the highest salaries.*

Eventually, we'll probably see several certification and licensing options for "software technologists"—today's coders—which will be the occupational equivalent of a physician's assistant in medicine or a certified technologist in engineering. This credential will stop short of giving software technologists full professional standing; they will not be able to sign off on a safety-critical software release or perform other activities reserved for the full professional engineers. But the certification will give software technologists a well-defined occupational credential. Software projects that are required to employ at least one professional engineer will still be able to employ certified technologists and other workers with no licensing or certification at all.

Specialization

In software development, most workers today are generalists. One moment they're architects; the next moment they are high-tech carpenters, pounding in each line of code, one at a time. The software occupation is beginning to stratify, and it is also beginning to specialize. You'll sometimes hear developers who are focused on technology discount expertise in technology areas they are unfamiliar with. One developer will say, "That developer is terrible. He has no idea what a port address is or how to write an interrupt service routine." The allegedly terrible developer might retort, "That other developer is terrible. She has no idea how to design a hierarchical query in

SQL or traverse a self-referential table." From the vantage point illustrated in Figure 11-2, this difference of opinion is easily resolved—some developers will narrowly focus on a specific technology to the exclusion of all else. Other developers with a broader software engineering education will be able to place each technology in an overall software engineering context—to view specific technologies as tools in a toolbox rather than as different ways of life.

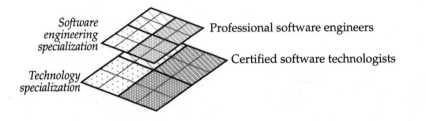

FIGURE 11-2   *In addition to its stratification, the software field is developing many different specialty areas at both the technology level and the software engineering level.*

As Figure 11-2 suggests, software technologists will specialize primarily on the basis of specific technologies. Various kinds of software technologist certification are already available from specific companies such as Microsoft, Novell, Oracle, and Apple Computer.

Specialization is beginning to occur in software engineering practices, but most software organizations are underspecialized. Capers Jones estimates that lack of software engineering specialization is currently causing low quality, schedule delays, and cost overruns in about 90 percent of all software organizations in the United States.

Twenty-five years ago, Fred Brooks proposed that programming teams be structured using a surgical team model. One chief programmer (the "surgeon") would write nearly all of the code, and other team members would be arrayed around the chief programmer in well-defined, specialized support roles. A test project in the late 1960s in which a team was structured this way demonstrated unprecedented productivity. Applying an additional quarter century of hindsight to this extraordinary project, it seems that its productivity might not have arisen from the specific surgical team structure but from the project's high degree of specialization. Studies about other software engineering practices have found that good training in specialty roles contributes more to effectiveness than the use of a particular practice does.

The more software workers a company employs, the greater the company's need for specialists—people whose jobs focus primarily on specialty areas rather than on general programming. In a small organization of 10 software employees, all 10 employees might be generalists, or there might be a relatively simple distinction between developer, tester, and management. In the handful of large organizations that employ 10,000 software workers, at least 20 percent of the employees will be specialists, and in some organizations specialization might run as high as 40 percent. Jones has encountered more than 100 different specializations in his organizational assessment work. Table 11-2 shows a sampling of those specializations and their representation in software companies of various sizes.

The specializations shown in this table are rough averages. The ratios of specialists to generalists will vary among different companies and different kinds of software organizations.

The benefits of specialization are not unique to software. A country doctor in practice for himself has to be a generalist, but large urban hospitals employ hundreds of specialists. Professional engineers specialize in particular fields, as do attorneys. Specialization is an attribute of a mature field.

Individual projects need specialization as much as organizations do. My company has created a technical project structure, partially based on the SWEBOK knowledge areas described in Chapter 8, that includes the following specialists on even our smallest projects:

◆ Configuration management lead

◆ Deployment lead

◆ Design lead

◆ Documentation lead

◆ Implementation lead

◆ Planning and tracking lead

◆ Program manager

◆ Quality assurance lead

◆ Requirements lead

In addition, other specialists operate at the company level:

◆ Evolution and maintenance lead

◆ Infrastructure (tools) lead

On most projects, these lead roles are part-time responsibilities, but we've found it useful to have a specific person assigned to look out for a project's interests in each of these areas. Each area requires specialized knowledge even on a 5–10 person project. More information on these lead areas, including recommended study programs for each one, is available from my company's web site at http://www.construx.com/profession/.

TABLE 11-2   APPROPRIATE SPECIALIZATION BY COMPANY SIZE

| | Number of Software Employees | | | | |
| | <10 | <100 | <1,000 | ≈10,000 | |
Proportion of Specialists	0%	10–25%	15–35%	20–40%	*Ratio to Generalists*
Specialty					
Architecture			X	X	1:75
Configuration control			X	X	1:30
Cost estimating			X	X	1:100
Customer support		X	X	X	1:25*
Database administration		X	X	X	1:25
Education and training				X	1:250
Function point counting			X	X	1:50
Human factors				X	1:250*
Information systems				X	1:250*
Integration				X	1:50
Maintenance and enhancement	O	X	X	X	1:4
Measurement			X	X	1:50
Network		X	X	X	1:50
Package acquisition				X	1:150
Performance				X	1:75
Process improvement				X	1:200
Planning				X	1:250*
Quality assurance	O	X	X	X	1:25
Requirements			X	X	1:50*
Reusability				X	1:100
Standards				X	1:300
Systems software support		X	X	X	1:30
Technical writing	O	X	X	X	1:15
Testing	O	X	X	X	1:8
Tool development				X	1:250*

Note: O indicates occasionally observed; X indicates usually observed.

* Estimated based on Jones's discussion, although he doesn't give a specific value.

Only Time Will Tell

Is increasing stratification and specialization a foregone conclusion, or will this prediction just look silly 20 years from now? Every complicated field eventually stratifies and breaks into specialty areas. This has already happened in medicine, law, and professional engineering, and the software community has begun moving in the same direction. A few jurisdictions have started licensing professional software engineers, which is a step toward stratification. Many companies offer certification in specific technologies, which is a step toward specialization. My crystal ball shows that, given sufficient time, software will become just as specialized and stratified as other mature fields. Whether that specialization will take 10 years, 20 years, or longer, my crystal ball doesn't show.

12
Hard Knocks

---◆---

"Natural abilities are like natural plants, that need pruning by study; and studies themselves do give forth directions too much at large, except they be bounded in by experience."
—*Francis Bacon*

---◆---

As I've hinted earlier, most software developers obtain their occupational education from the school of hard knocks. Experience can be a good teacher, but it is also a slow and expensive one.

A common lament among experienced software developers is that colleges don't teach students the skills they need to perform effectively on the job. An examination of current demographics in software developer education and training seems to bear this out. I argued in Chapter 4 that

North American universities are providing educations in computer science rather than in software engineering. I left many of the implications of those different educational programs unexplored, and I would like to explore them here.

During the past few years, industry has become less and less satisfied with university output. Capers Jones points out that, since the mid-1980s, large corporations in the United States have had more in-house instructors teaching software engineering topics than all universities combined. Many of those corporations offer more comprehensive software engineering course catalogs than virtually any university catalog.

The Boeing Company studied the computer science curricula of more than 200 universities in the United States. It wanted to identify programs that were producing graduates with the skills needed to perform satisfactorily at Boeing. It found that only about half the programs were accredited by the Computer Science Accreditation Board (CSAB), and that only about half of the accredited programs were producing graduates that met its requirements. Some of the programs are more practically oriented, but they become more practical by teaching software engineering under the guise of computer science, which diffuses their focus on true computer science.

For engineering jobs, however, Boeing will accept applications from graduates of any program accredited by the Accreditation Board for Engineering and Technology (ABET). Boeing does not accept applications for engineering jobs from graduates of unaccredited schools. This suggests that computer science curriculum and accreditation standards are of questionable value to industry. A significant percentage of programs do not meet industry's needs. In contrast, the value of engineering curriculum and accreditation is so consistent that companies such as Boeing can hire from accredited engineering schools without screening any university programs.

The questionable relevance of computer science education to industry provides one explanation for the decline and stagnation in undergraduate computer science degrees that students have earned during the past 15 years. As Figure 12-1 shows, the number of undergraduate computer science degrees has declined from a high of about 42,000 annually to a current level of about 24,000.

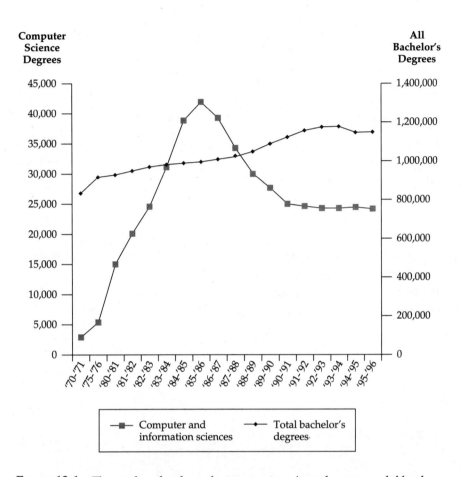

FIGURE 12-1   *The number of undergraduate computer science degrees awarded has been declining or level in recent years. (Source: National Center for Education Statistics, 1998 Digest of Educational Statistics, Document number NCES 1999036, 1999.)*

The conventional explanation for this decline is that students find computer science dull. I don't find computer science dull, and I don't find the conventional wisdom persuasive. The real answer has been staring us in the face for many years: the number of students obtaining computer science degrees has declined because education in computer science has become increasingly irrelevant to job-market requirements. Students know they can get jobs without computer science degrees, and employers don't universally value them. The old educational system isn't working, and it's time to do something about it.

Development of Professional Engineers

As I've argued throughout the book, engineering makes a good model for a profession of software development, and the professional development path that engineers follow does too.

Professional engineering requires in-depth knowledge of both theory and practice. As Figure 12-2 illustrates, a professional engineer first obtains a bachelor of science degree from an accredited engineering school. An engineer then takes a Fundamentals of Engineering (FE) exam, which is sometimes called an Engineer in Training (EIT) exam. After passing the exam, the engineer works for several years under the guidance of a professional engineer. At the end of that period, the engineer takes a professional engineering exam in his or her specialty area—such as civil, electrical, or chemical engineering. After passing that exam, the engineer's state, province, or territory will issue a professional engineer license, and a new professional engineer will be created.

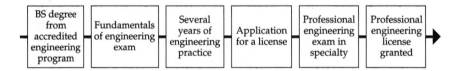

FIGURE 12-2   *The occupational development path that professional engineers follow includes education, training, and experience. This provides a good model for professional development in software engineering.*

Striking the right balance between theory and practice in software engineering education depends on making a distinction between education and training. Education seeks to instill qualities in students that will enable them to respond effectively to diverse intellectual challenges. It focuses on general knowledge and includes development of critical thinking skills. Training provides specific skills and knowledge that can be applied immediately. Education is strategic; training is tactical.

The most common kind of occupational development for software developers today is training. It tends to be reactive and is provided—just in time—in the specific technologies that a developer needs to know to work on a specific project. Education in longer lasting software engineering principles is almost completely absent from the picture. As I suggested in Chapter 11, some people claim that software development has become too specialized and fragmented to be amenable to standardized education. It is too fragmented for standardized training, but not for standardized education.

First Steps

Graduate-level programs in software engineering have existed for about 20 years, but undergraduate programs are still in their infancy, especially in North America. Seattle University awarded the world's first software engineering master's degree in 1982. The Department of Computer Science at the University of Sheffield in the United Kingdom introduced an undergraduate degree program in software engineering in 1988. Rochester Institute of Technology (RIT) initiated the first undergraduate software engineering program in the United States, admitting freshmen in 1996.

At present, about 25 software engineering master's programs are offered in the United States. A handful are offered in Canada, the United Kingdom, Australia, and other countries. As of fall 1999, RIT's bachelor program will be joined by bachelor's programs at Auburn University, Milwaukee School of Engineering, and Montana Tech. In Canada, bachelor's programs are offered by Concordia University, McMaster University, Memorial University of Newfoundland, and University of Ottawa. Several other North American universities are actively considering adding programs. At least 13 universities offer undergraduate programs in the United Kingdom and at least 6 more offer them in Australia.

RIT has been working with the IEEE Computer Society, the ACM, and ABET to develop a program that can be accredited as an engineering program in the United States. Figure 12-3 shows the courses required in RIT's program.

RIT's Software Engineering Curriculum

First year

- Freshman Seminar (1)*
- Computer Science I, II, III (12)
  (engineering problem solving)
- Calculus I, II, III (12)
- College Chemistry I (4)
- University Physics I, II & Lab (10)
- English Composition (4)
- Liberal Arts (8)
- Physical Education Electives (0)

Second year

- Engineering of Software Subsystems (4)
- Computer Science IV (4)
  (data structures)
- Professional Communications (4)
- Introduction to Software Engineering (4)
- Assembly Language Programming (4)
- Introduction to Digital Systems (4)
- Differential Equations (4)
- Discrete Mathematics I, II (8)
- University Physics III & Lab (5)
- Liberal Arts (8)
- Physical Education Electives (0)

Third, fourth, and fifth years

- Principles of Software Architecture (4)
- Formal Methods of Specification & Design (4)
- Software Requirements & Specification (4)
- Software Engineering Project I, II (8)
- Software Engineering Electives** (20)
- Scientific Applications Programming (4)
- Programming Language Concepts (4)
- Computer Architecture (4)
- Human Factors (4)
- Probability & Statistics (4)
- Application Domain Electives*** (12)
- Free Elective (4)
- Liberal Arts (18)
- Cooperative Education (5 quarters required)

---

* *Quarter hours are shown in parentheses.*
** *Students must choose five of the following six courses: Principles of Concurrent Software Systems,*
Principles of Distributed Software Systems, Principles of Information Systems Design, Software Metrics,
Software Verification and Validation, and Software Process.
*** *Each student must complete a three-course sequence in an application domain related to software engineering.*
Current domains include Electrical Engineering, Industrial Engineering, Mechanical Engineering,
Communications and Networks, Embedded Systems, and Commercial Applications.

FIGURE 12-3   *RIT's undergraduate software engineering program requires courses in computer science, communications, liberal arts, and software engineering.*

RIT's program contains some courses from the computer science department (for example, Computer Science I, I, III, and IV). It also contains several courses that you wouldn't normally find in a computer science program including Software Requirements and Specification, Software Engineering Project I and II, Human Factors, Software Metrics, Software Process, and Software Verification and Validation. It also requires five quarters of cooperative education—in other words, a student must obtain significant experience with industrial practice before earning a degree. This sort of experience requirement is a hallmark of an engineering program. Computer science programs can require industry experience, but only at the expense of diluting their emphasis on pure science.

One interesting aspect of RIT's program is its length—five years. During the mid-1900s, engineering undergraduate degrees were usually five-year programs. Later, various pressures led universities to shorten their programs to four years. Teaching software engineering as an undergraduate degree in four years may be impractical, especially using the RIT model in which students spend a year gaining experience in industry. Five-year programs may become the norm for undergraduate software engineering.

Accreditation

Accreditation of university programs is required to maintain high standards of software engineering education. Accreditation guarantees that students who graduate from an accredited program will have acquired the basic knowledge of the field. It also ensures that they share a common working vocabulary and common assumptions about good ways to do their work. In the United States, engineering programs are accredited by ABET, which won't certify a program until it has graduated its first class. Many universities are watching RIT to see if its program receives ABET accreditation when it graduates its first class in 2001. If RIT's program receives its accreditation, several universities will probably begin offering software engineering undergraduate programs almost immediately.

One difference between computer science and engineering is the accreditation requirements that faculty who teach those subjects must meet. The CSAB criteria for accrediting computer science programs in the United States require faculty to make "scholarly contributions" to computer science, but they don't require industry experience. In contrast, the ABET criteria for accrediting engineering programs in the United States state that "nonacademic engineering experience" and registration as professional engineers should be considered in faculty evaluations. The Canadian Engineering Accreditation Board uses similar criteria. In professional education, it is important that many of the teachers be qualified and working in the profession—doctors teach doctors, lawyers teach lawyers, and so on.

The differences between engineering and computer science accreditation criteria do not imply that one approach is right and the other is wrong. The objectives of each are simply different. Science programs prepare students to conduct research; engineering programs prepare students to participate in industry. Software has a pervasive need for people who have been well prepared to work in industry. Undergraduate degree programs in software engineering should prove to be popular both with students and with the companies that hire them.

Polishing the Badge

After a professional has obtained initial education, gained some experience, and received a license, most professions impose a continuing education requirement. The specific requirements for each profession vary from state to state. In Washington state, certified public accountants are required to earn 80 continuing professional education credits during the two years preceding renewal of their certificates. Attorneys must obtain 15 continuing legal education credits each year. Physicians in New Mexico must obtain 150 hours of continuing education every three years. Engineers in Washington state do not have any continuing education requirements; engineers in some other states do.

Continuing education helps to ensure that professionals stay current in their fields, which is especially important in fields with rapidly changing knowledge such as medicine and software engineering. If professionals revert to learning their lessons only from the school of hard knocks after completing their initial education, time will render their education less and less meaningful.

Continuing education requirements can be focused so that professionals are required to learn about important developments in their fields. If software engineering ever does discover a new silver bullet, continuing education requirements can ensure that all licensed or certified software engineers learn about it.

Some Perspective

The field of software development is only about 50 years old. In that time, software has managed to revolutionize modern life to such an extent that we would have a hard time imagining life without software. As has been the case in other engineering disciplines, software practice has led software theory much of the time, and universities have not always kept up. On the other hand, practice has also had trouble keeping up with some of the theory because the general level of education in software engineering techniques has been so poor. Without the university infrastructure in place, transferring proven theories into practice is difficult.

Educational programs for software engineering that are modeled on traditional engineering programs are just right. They will produce graduates more useful to industry than computer science programs do. They will allow computer science programs to heal their currently split personalities and focus more on science. And a software engineering education will be less painful for all involved than equivalent education from the school of hard knocks.

13

The Professional's Code

---◆---

"Although there is a little bit of Peter Pan in each of us,
maturity brings with it the desire to contribute to the
communal welfare. The fulfillment of this yearning,
I repeat, provides the engineer with his primary
existential pleasure."
—Samuel C. Florman

---◆---

One sign of a mature profession is the presence of a code of ethics or a standard of professional conduct. Legally, professionals are held to a higher standard of work performance than nonprofessionals performing work in the same field. If your friend the plumber tells you to take Alka

Seltzer for a stomachache and the problem turns out to be a ruptured appendix, the plumber hasn't done anything unethical. If your friend were a doctor and told you the same thing without conducting an adequate examination, giving the advice would be an unethical act.

A code of ethics establishes the standard of conduct for each profession. Certified public accountants are required to pass a three-hour exam covering their code of ethics. Lawyers are required to pass a half-day ethics exam. In mature professions, workers can be disbarred or lose their licenses for serious violations of their ethics codes.

A Code for Coders

Software development survived for many years without a widely accepted code of ethics. In the late 1990s, a joint committee of the ACM and IEEE Computer Society began developing a code of ethics for software engineering. The code underwent several drafts and was reviewed by practicing software developers worldwide. In 1998 the Software Engineering Code of Ethics and Professional Practice was adopted by both the ACM and IEEE Computer Society. The short version, shown in Figure 13-1, contains two primary goals stated in its preamble and eight specific principles. A much more detailed version of the Code is available from the IEEE Computer Society web site at www.computer.org.

The Code warrants some examination. The first overriding goal of the Code is that "Software engineers shall commit themselves to making the analysis, specification, design, development, testing, and maintenance of software a beneficial and respected profession." In other words, one function of the Code is to foster the development of the software engineering profession itself—which implicitly acknowledges that software engineering is *not yet* a "beneficial and respected profession." Once the profession has become more mature, this language may be revised to say that software engineers will "maintain" or "enhance" the respected profession rather than "make" it.

The second overriding goal is that software engineers have a "commitment to the health, safety, and welfare of the public." This goal is consistent with the idea that engineers more commonly have a duty to society than to specific individuals. Other engineering codes of ethics similarly emphasize the importance of protecting public welfare.

The Software Engineering Code of Ethics and Professional Practice

Software engineers shall commit themselves to making the analysis, specification, design, development, testing, and maintenance of software a beneficial and respected profession. In accordance with their commitment to the health, safety, and welfare of the public, software engineers shall adhere to the following eight principles:

1. **Public** Software engineers shall act consistently with the public interest.
2. **Client and Employer** Software engineers shall act in a manner that is in the best interests of their client and employer consistent with the public interest.
3. **Product** Software engineers shall ensure that their products and related modifications meet the highest professional standards possible.
4. **Judgement** Software engineers shall maintain integrity and independence in their professional judgment.
5. **Management** Software engineering managers and leaders shall subscribe to and promote an ethical approach to the management of software development and maintenance.
6. **Profession** Software engineers shall advance the integrity and reputation of the profession consistent with the public interest.
7. **Colleagues** Software engineers shall be fair to and supportive of their colleagues.
8. **Self** Software engineers shall participate in lifelong learning regarding the practice of their profession and shall promote an ethical approach to the practice of the profession.

FIGURE 13-1   *The Software Engineering Code of Ethics and Professional Practice. This code has been adopted by both the ACM and IEEE Computer Society and provides ethical and professional guidance for software engineers.*

The two goals just discussed are primary, and the eight specific principles should be interpreted as supporting them. In the following discussion of the specific principles, I've provided my interpretation.

1. Public   Software engineers shall accept full responsibility for their work and approve software only if they have a well-founded belief that it is safe, meets specifications, passes appropriate tests, and is ultimately to the public good. Software engineers shall disclose any actual or potential danger to specific persons, the public, or the environment.

2. Client and employer   Clients and employers are directly affected by software engineers' work, and so software engineers need to protect their clients' and employers' interests, except when those interests conflict with a greater public interest. Software engineers shall provide services only within their areas of expertise. They shall protect confidential information and not accept outside work or promote interests that are detrimental to their clients or employers. They shall not use software that was obtained illegally or unethically. If they think a project is likely to fail, they shall report the evidence that leads them to believe that to their employer or client.

3. Product   In all their work, software engineers shall strive for high quality, acceptable costs, and reasonable schedules. They shall ensure that tradeoffs among these are clear to their employers and clients. They shall provide assessments of the uncertainties contained in their estimates. Software engineers shall follow relevant professional standards. They shall ensure that software has been adequately reviewed and tested before it is released to the public.

4. Judgment   True professionals have both the right and the duty to exercise their professional judgment independently—to adhere to a high professional standard even when it conflicts with their self-interest or their clients' or employers' interests. Software engineers shall endorse only products that they have adequately reviewed and objectively agree with. They shall not engage in illegal or dishonest activities such as bribery, double billing, or working for two parties that have conflicting interests without fully disclosing the conflict of interest.

5. Management   Software engineering managers shall abide by the same professional standards as other software engineers, including the provisions of the Code of Ethics. Software engineering managers shall treat their employees fairly and honestly. They shall assign work to people qualified to perform the work, tempered with the goal of furthering each employee's education and experience. They shall ensure realistic quantitative estimates of cost, schedule, staffing, quality, and other outcomes of projects they work on.

6. Profession Software engineers shall help to advance software engineering as a profession. They shall promote public knowledge of software engineering. They shall create a work environment that supports the Code and refuse to work for organizations that are in conflict with it. They shall report significant violations of the Code to colleagues, managers, or other appropriate authorities.

7. Colleagues Software engineers shall help other software engineers follow the Code of Ethics. They shall treat each other fairly and provide assistance in others' professional development. In situations that require expertise outside their areas of competence, they shall call upon the assistance of other professionals who have appropriate expertise.

8. Self Software engineers shall make self-education a career-long priority. They shall maintain current knowledge of developments in software requirements, design, construction, maintenance, testing, and management. They shall maintain current knowledge of standards and laws relevant to their work.

Benefits of the Code of Ethics

A recognized code of ethics provides broad support for a true profession of software engineering. It establishes minimum performance expectations. It gives employers and clients confidence about the professional standards and character of engineers who adhere to it.

The Code provides a way for companies to show their support for professional software engineering. When a company commits to the Code, it commits to providing an environment in which professional software engineers can make ethical conduct a priority without jeopardizing their advancement within that company. This is beneficial both to the company and the software engineers it employs. The company attracts software engineers with high professional standards, and the engineers find professional fulfillment in an environment that appreciates their high standards.

The strongest benefit of the Code is the guidance it provides for software engineers' ethical and professional conduct, guidance that has been sorely lacking. Consider the following cases.

Death-march projects   Without a code of ethics, software engineers who believe a project's schedule is unachievable might debate whether to report that to their client or manager. With the Code, software engineers who think a project is likely to fail will know that they should collect evidence and document their concerns. The Code says they have a professional duty to report their concerns promptly to their employer or client.

Low-ball bidding   The practice of submitting unrealistically low bids to clients is common in the software industry. Software developers might not like the practice, but many feel uncomfortable defying their bosses by refusing to support a low-ball bid. The Code states that software engineers should ensure that estimates are realistic and should not endorse documents unless they agree with them. It also calls upon software engineers to make software engineering a respected profession, a goal that is undermined by participating in low-ball bidding. The ethical software engineer should refuse to endorse low-ball bids.

Code-and-fix development   Uninformed clients and managers sometimes insist that software developers engage in code-and-fix development. Software developers know that code-and-fix development is ineffective, but after repeated battles with clients and managers, many finally sigh and say, "I'll let this company get the results it deserves." Use of code-and-fix development, however, is inconsistent with a software engineer's ethical duty to produce high-quality products for acceptable costs and according to reasonable schedules. Continued use of code-and-fix development also undermines the advancement of software engineering as a profession, and ethical software engineers should refuse to use code-and-fix development.

Knowledge stagnation   Keeping up to date in software engineering can be time-consuming, and many software developers don't even try. One publisher reported that the average software developer reads less than one professional book each year and subscribes to no professional magazines. This might not seem like an ethical issue, but it is certainly a *professional practice* issue. A person cannot perform at a professional level without keeping current in the knowledge of the profession. A person who doesn't want to engage in ongoing self-education can continue to perform software work at some level, but according to The Software Engineering Code of Ethics and Professional Practice a person cannot be a *professional* software engineer without participating in lifelong learning.

Without a code of ethics, software engineers must rely solely on their individual judgments to resolve ethical dilemmas. Engineers who act consistently with the Code will know that the consensus of engineers is behind them; they don't have to take their ethical stands in isolation.

Some situations will be less clear-cut than the examples just listed. The interests of a client may come into conflict with the public interest. Or the interests of an employer might conflict with the interests of a software engineering colleague. The Code cannot foresee every possible ethical dilemma, but it calls for software engineers to use their best ethical judgment to adhere to its spirit, considering it as a whole.

Growing Up

The Code provides a way of educating the public, including clients and upper management, about what to expect from professional software engineers. Of course, the Code is meaningful only if employers and clients can reasonably expect that software engineering professionals actually follow it. Every profession needs a way to discipline workers who fail to live up to the relevant professional standards. Without enforcement, workers who don't live up to those standards can gradually erode the credibility of the profession. At the present time, neither the IEEE Computer Society, the ACM, nor any other organization has any meaningful authority to enforce the Code. Compliance with it is voluntary. In the long run, however, software engineering will follow the same path as other professions; full professional standing and adherence to the Code will become a package deal. The Code will be enforced, which will be beneficial to individual software engineers, their employers and clients, and the public.

Samuel Florman said, "Maturity brings with it the desire to contribute to the communal welfare." Florman was referring to individuals, but his statement might just as well have referred to the occupation of software engineering. The Software Engineering Code of Ethics and Professional Practice, which emphasizes responsibility to the profession and contribution to society as a whole, is one indication that software engineering is beginning to grow up.

14

Alchemy

---◆---

*"Q: What are the most exciting/promising software
engineering ideas or techniques on the horizon?
A: I don't think that the most promising ideas are on the
horizon. They are already here and have been here for years
but are not being used properly."*
—*David L. Parnas, interview in*
Software Engineering Notes

---◆---

How to transmute base metals into gold? That is the perennial question
from would-be Midases everywhere. Software engineering is in a
unique position to realize the alchemic dream by hastening the adoption of
practices that are well understood and that were proven beneficial many
years ago but are still not commonly used. We are in a position to transform
the lead of average practice into the gold of best practice.

Why Technology Transfer Is Needed

The process by which innovations move from research settings into common practice is called "technology transfer," or "diffusion." An innovation can be a technology (such as UNIX), a best practice (such as design inspections), or any other invention that helps practitioners work more effectively. The software engineering field already has good practices for project planning and management, requirements engineering, design, construction, quality assurance, and process improvement. The problem is that few practitioners know about these practices, and even fewer use them. Table 14-1 lists some examples of innovations with which leading software organizations have accumulated a great deal of experience, that are usually successful, and that— as far as I can tell from my consulting experience and various published industry reports—are used by only a slim minority of software organizations.

TABLE 14-1   RARELY USED SOFTWARE INNOVATIONS

Innovations	Year First Described in Print or First Commercially Available
Project Planning and Management	
Automated estimation tools	1973
Evolutionary delivery	1988
Measurement	1977
Productivity environments	1984
Risk management planning	1981
Requirements Engineering	
Change board	1978
Throwaway user-interface prototyping	1975
JAD sessions	1985
Design	
Information hiding	1972
Design for change	1979
Construction	
Source-code control	1980
Incremental integration	1979

(continued)

TABLE 14-1   RARELY USED SOFTWARE INNOVATIONS *continued*

Innovations	Year First Described in Print or First Commercially Available
Quality Assurance	
Branch-coverage testing	1979
Inspections	1976
Process Improvement	
Software Engineering Institute's Capability Maturity Model for Software	1987
Software Engineering Process Groups	1989

Researchers have found that it typically takes 10–15 years for innovations to flow down the technology-transfer stream into common practice. If that's the case, the software industry's technology transfer cycle is seriously broken. Most of the innovations listed in Table 14-1 have been described in print for 15 years or more. Why aren't they being used?

Diffusion of Innovation

The way in which innovations are diffused into common practice has been studied extensively. The seminal work on technology transfer is Everett M. Rogers' *Diffusion of Innovation*, which was originally published in 1962. In the fourth edition, published in 1995, Rogers comments that more than 3,500 books and articles about diffusion were published between his first edition and his fourth.

Rogers describes how innovations are adopted based on categorization of the adopters. The adopters include Innovators, Early Adopters, Early Majority, Late Majority, and Laggards. Figure 14-1 shows both the relative sizes of these groups and the sequence in which they adopt innovations.

Innovators are adventurous. They want to try out new technologies, no matter how rash, daring, or risky. They can cope with a high degree of uncertainty brought on by adopting unstable new technologies and practices. Because they court high risk, they fail frequently. As a result, they may not be respected by people in the other categories.

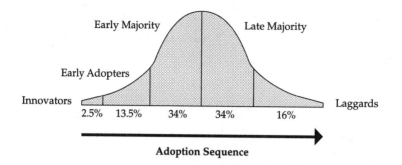

Adoption Sequence

FIGURE 14-1   *Innovations are diffused over time. The groups that adopt an innovation have different needs and use different criteria to evaluate it. (Source: adapted from Everett,* Diffusion of Innovations, 4th ed., 1995.)

Early Adopters are the respected opinion leaders in their organizations. They are ahead of the majority in adopting innovations, but just far enough ahead to serve as role models for other adopters. They adopt innovations later than Innovators do.

Adopters in the *Early Majority* are more deliberate about taking up innovations than Early Adopters, and they are one of the two largest groups. Their decision period is longer than the Early Adopters. They follow the lead established by the Early Adopters and adopt innovations later—sometimes significantly later.

Adopters in the *Late Majority* are skeptical of innovations. They are cautious and adopt innovations only after many others have already adopted them. They are not convinced that the innovations are better than existing practices or technologies, or that the innovations apply to them. Adoption may depend on pressure from peers.

Laggards are the last to adopt innovations and tend to focus more on the past than on the future. They are extremely cautious in adopting innovations.

Rogers' work was extended in the mid-1990s by Geoffrey Moore in *Crossing the Chasm*. Moore pointed out that the differences in decision-making styles between the adopter groups create gaps between them. A message that persuades Innovators to adopt something new would not necessarily persuade Early Adopters.

Moore's most significant insight was that not all the gaps are equal. As Figure 14-2 illustrates, Moore believes that the gap between the Early Adopters and the Early Majority is much wider than the gaps between the other groups, so wide that he calls it a chasm.

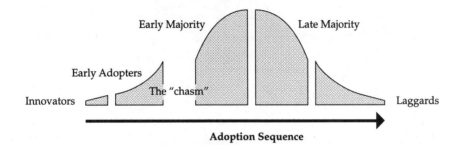

FIGURE 14-2   *One difficulty with technology transfer is crossing the chasm that separates the needs of the Early Adopters from the needs of the Early Majority. (Source: adapted from Moore,* Crossing the Chasm, *1991.)*

Some Tough Questions

One reason that new innovations move into practice slowly is that some of them don't work very well in practice. Not all innovations are useful, and the Early Majority, Late Majority, and Laggards have some good reasons for being cautious. When presented with an innovation, they ask tough questions like these:

◆   Do experimental results prove conclusively that the innovation will work in practice?

◆   Are successes a result of the innovation itself, or might they be the result of the people using it?

◆   Is the innovation complete, or does it need to be adapted or extended before it can be applied?

◆   Does the innovation have significant overhead (training, documentation) that offset its value in the long run?

◆   If the innovation was developed in a research setting, does it apply to real-world problems?

◆   Does the innovation generally slow down the programmers?

◆   Can the innovation be misapplied?

◆   Is information available about the risks involved with using the innovation?

◆   Does the innovation include information about how to integrate it with existing practices?

◆   Must the innovation be applied in its entirety to realize significant benefits?

How many software engineering practices could withstand such questioning? Several have been studied enough, and people who diligently read software engineering journals know the answers. But the study results haven't been widely disseminated to rank-and-file practitioners and, as a result, the software engineering practices described in Table 14-1 are stuck on the left side of the chasm. Early Adopters have been using many of those techniques for 10 years or more, while the groups that adopt innovations later are largely unaware of them. The numbers from Rogers' categories are close to the numbers of projects that use code-and-fix development—about 75 percent of projects are still using the code-and-fix approach, and about 85 percent of adopters fall onto the right side of the chasm.

Why is this? In Rogers' framework, one reason that innovations are diffused to Innovators and Early Adopters more quickly is that Innovators and Early Adopters tend to have more resources—they are in better positions to afford costly mistakes. Later adopters are more cautious partly because they aren't as resource rich. As I mentioned in Chapter 3, however, the scarce resource isn't money—it's *time*. Lagging-edge practices such as code-and-fix development are associated with significant schedule overruns. The overtime that usually accompanies such overruns doesn't leave time for investigating and adopting more effective innovations.

Where's the Risk?

The conventional wisdom is that if you're a risk taker, you'll be to the left of the chasm. If you're risk averse, you'll be to the right of the chasm. But this conventional wisdom doesn't apply very well to current software engineering.

As Figure 14-3 illustrates, practices from Table 14-1 are being used by Innovators and Early Adopters, but haven't crossed the chasm. The figure also shows a few other practices to illustrate how software engineering innovations are diffusing. For example, the Software Engineering Institute (SEI)'s SW-CMM seems to have crossed the chasm, but it is barely into Early Majority territory. The well-known waterfall lifecycle model is in Late Majority territory, and code-and-fix development is well into Laggard territory. (It might be misleading to say it's in Laggard territory, because it isn't really an innovation—it's the technique used by default.)

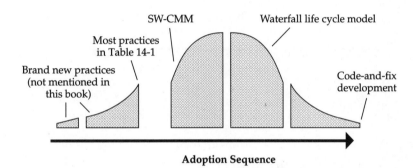

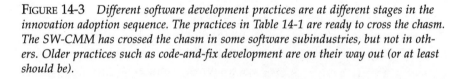

FIGURE 14-3   *Different software development practices are at different stages in the innovation adoption sequence. The practices in Table 14-1 are ready to cross the chasm. The SW-CMM has crossed the chasm in some software subindustries, but not in others. Older practices such as code-and-fix development are on their way out (or at least should be).*

The state of the art in software development has advanced by leaps and bounds during the past 20 years, but we still find many organizations using practices that are 10–20 years out of date—and which could be replaced by better practices. The industry is confronting a problem of slow diffusion. I've mentioned elsewhere that organizations that use these old practices face high risk of cost overruns, schedule overruns, and project cancellations. I repeat that fact here to emphasize that organizations occupying one of the later adopter roles in the software field *are not currently minimizing risk.* Just as it's possible to spend more on repairs for an old car that keeps breaking down than on payments for a newer one, it's possible to incur more risk by using out-of-date software development practices than by moving to newer, better practices.

Where do you want to be on the technology transfer cycle? As Figure 14-4 illustrates, on the far left, the risk of promising but as-yet-unproven innovations is justified because the innovations might yield high payoffs. On the far right, the risk from using outdated practices is equally high, but you don't have the potential for high payoffs, and so the risk isn't justified.

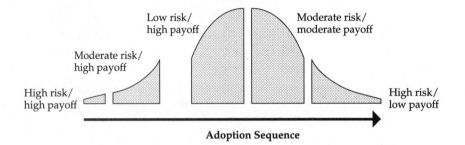

FIGURE 14-4   *The traditional innovation risk/reward payoff has gotten out of balance. Both extremes of the innovation adoption curve present high risk.*

The software industry is in an unusual technology-transfer situation. Many innovative practices that have proven their value, such as those in Table 14-1, have congregated on the left brink of the chasm. They are ready to cross for organizations that are willing to kick their addiction to code-and-fix development and other kinds of software fool's gold. This situation is unusual because innovations as well developed and proven as these would typically already have crossed the chasm. Innovations at this stage in the adoption sequence are usually less well developed, and the risk of being an Early Adopter is usually higher. The current state of the software industry is as if leading-edge doctors had tested penicillin, found it be to effective, and integrated it into their practices, only to have 75 percent of doctors continue to use leeches and mustard poultices. If you're still using leeches and poultices at the beginning of the twenty-first century, you're taking on more risk by refusing innovations than by adopting them.

If your organization is currently in the Early Majority, Late Majority, or Laggard categories, you can lower your risk by adopting some of the modern practices listed in Table 14-1. As I've said before, using code-and-fix development is risky. Using the waterfall model is risky. Adopting the SW-CMM is somewhat risky, but not as risky as using the older practices. Industry experience cited throughout this book shows this claim to be true. The challenge is diffusing the message into the field.

County Extension Agents

The United States' agricultural extension service is regarded as the most successful diffusion program in the world. As one author said, "It is impossible for anyone to speak ten words about diffusion without two of them being 'agricultural extension'." The service consists of three parts:

◆ *Research Subsystem*   Research professors at agricultural experiment stations in each of the 50 states. These professors produce the innovations that are later diffused.

◆ *State Extension Specialists*   Individuals who link the research work to the County Extension Agents.

◆ *County Extension Agents*   Individuals who work with farmers and other people at the local level, helping them to choose innovations appropriate to their needs. They answer practitioners' tough questions such as, "Is the innovation complete, or does it need to be adapted or extended before it can be applied?" and "Are the innovation's successes a result of the innovation itself, or might they be the result of the people using it?"

The agricultural program places a strong emphasis on cooperation among its three parts. Research professors are rewarded for publishing research results in a form directly useful to farmers. State Extension Specialists are evaluated based on how well they relate their technical knowledge to farmers' problems.

The program's annual investment in diffusing agricultural innovation is approximately equal to the annual investment in agricultural research, which makes the program unique. No other federal program spends more than a few percent of its budget on diffusion, and no other program is as successful at changing common practice.

Experience in the software industry provides some confirmation of the value of emphasizing diffusion. One of the best organizations in software, NASA's Software Engineering Laboratory, has found that packaging the results of its measurement and analysis program into guidebooks and training courses is a critical part of its award-winning process improvement program.

Diffusion of innovation in software is needed, and the software industry does have the beginnings of a diffusion program. The SEI was created with federal funding to "provide leadership in advancing the state of the practice of software engineering to improve the quality of systems that depend on software." The SEI essentially performs the role that the Research Subsystem does in the agricultural extension model. At about 300 employees to serve 1.8 million software workers, however, the SEI program is in the beginning stages compared to the agriculture program, which employs about 17,000 people to serve 3.8 million agricultural workers.

Everett Rogers points out that many government agencies have tried to copy the agricultural extension model but have failed because, among other reasons, they didn't establish local-level change agents analogous to the County Extension Agents. Rogers' analysis goes a long way toward explaining the limited impact that the SEI has had so far on commercial practice. The SEI was created by the United States Department of Defense, and the documents and materials it has produced have had a strong DOD flavor. Not surprisingly, the industries that benefited earliest from the SEI's technology transfer role were military contractors and government agencies.

The software industry has many subindustries with specific needs and specialized vocabularies. These subindustries include aerospace, business systems, web development, software products, games, medical devices, systems software, computer manufacturing, and embedded systems. Combine the failure to translate software engineering innovations into terms familiar to each subindustry with the common lack of in-depth education in software engineering, and you have a formula for slow progress.

Practitioners won't adopt innovations until they get their tough questions answered in terms they can relate to. For software technology transfer to work effectively, either the government or private industry needs to fund roles similar to the State Extension Specialist and County Extension Agent. Software-project needs don't vary from county to county as farming needs do. But they do vary from subindustry to subindustry, and software engineering might very well benefit from extension specialists who can link general software research to specific subindustries.

Other developments that will help speed technology transfer include the elements of a mature profession I have discussed throughout this book: undergraduate educational programs in software engineering, certification and licensing standards, requirements for ongoing professional education, organizational certification, and a professional code of ethics.

The Humbling Nature of Progress

A few years ago I traveled to a rural town, not to meet with a County Extension Agent, but to meet with a software engineering colleague I hadn't previously met in person. Immediately after we introduced ourselves, he asked me, "Writing a book the size of *Code Complete* was awfully audacious for someone your age, wouldn't you agree?"

Much as I like being called audacious, I would not agree. My writing of *Code Complete* is representative of the way that knowledge is transferred from generation to generation in scientific and engineering fields, and of the way it ultimately advances. Early pioneers in software engineering such as Victor Basili, Barry Boehm, Larry Constantine, Bill Curtis, Tom DeMarco, Tom Gilb, Capers Jones, Harlan Mills, David Parnas, and others struggle to create leading-edge concepts from ill-defined bits of knowledge. They work against backgrounds of erroneous theories, conflicting data, and sketchy or nonexistent previous work. Others have the benefit of reading the early pioneers' work, and they are not exposed to all the false turns and mistaken assumptions. Newcomers who haven't struggled to come up with original concepts themselves are sometimes better able to explain the work of the early pioneers than the pioneers themselves were. Larry Constantine performed the original work that led to structured design. Ed Yourdon explained Constantine's structured design work, but that explanation was still inaccessible to most readers. It wasn't until Meilir Page-Jones explained Yourdon's explanation that Constantine's work finally became accessible to the average practitioner, and the concepts were diffused into common practice. Later, the concepts of structured design were absorbed into object-oriented design. And the diffusion cycle began again.

Eventually, knowledge that took early pioneers whole careers to master will be taught to undergraduate college students in a few semesters. It took me three and a half years to write *Code Complete*. Someday, a software developer even more "audacious" than I was will write a better book in only a few months. That is the way that lead turns slowly into gold in software engineering, and that is the way it should be.

Epilogue

---◆---

"Success is the ability to go from one failure to another
with no loss of enthusiasm."
—*Winston Churchill*

---◆---

Software development has been fighting the sticky grip of the tar pit for a long time. We are on the brink of fixing many familiar problems, but we haven't actually fixed them yet. We need to continue working on several fronts—instituting widespread undergraduate education, licensing professional software engineers, establishing software engineering certification programs, and thoroughly diffusing best practices into the industry. The software engineering field will need at least 10–15 years to create a true profession of software engineering. What can you do in the meantime?

If you are a software client, I hope this book has convinced you that the mistakes you have seen so many times are avoidable. You can support effective software development practices by giving your business to software companies that demonstrate a commitment to software *engineering*. The clearest sign of such commitment at this time is SW-CMM assessment at Level 2, 3, 4, or 5, as described in Chapter 7.

If you are a software manager, I hope that you, too, have been convinced that common software development problems can be avoided; they won't be avoided without your support. I hope that you will commit your organization to software process improvement. Provide your staff with training in software engineering principles as well as in new technologies. Support your staff's attempts to avoid code-and-fix development, and learn to recognize real signs of progress on your projects, not the fool's-gold signs described in Chapter 2. Make explicit tradeoffs that favor development of long-term capabilities, even at the expense of short-term business objectives. If you're not willing to make those trade-offs, significant improvements will be elusive.

investments

If you are a software developer, I hope that you will join the effort to create a true profession of software engineering. You might begin by making a personal commitment to professional self-education. You can use a guided list of self-study materials, such as the one available from my company's web site, to move yourself from square zero to professional software engineering. You need knowledge of specific technologies to do your job, but you need knowledge of software engineering principles to do your job *well*. Time spent learning software engineering principles is a good investment because much of what you learn will last your whole career.

Current information about the state of the profession—including what you can do to help—is available from my company's web site at http://www.construx.com/profession/.

Notes

Introduction

Page

ix "Today, that part's function": Andrew Pollack, "For Coders, a Code of Conduct," *New York Times*, 3 May 1999.

ix "Their managers think": Private communication with the author.

ix "They don't know that the typical": The Standish Group, "Charting the Seas of Information Technology," Dennis, MA: The Standish Group, 1994.

ix "The software delighted": Buford D. Tackett III and Buddy Van Doren, "Process Control for Error Free Software: A Software Success Story," *IEEE Software*, May 1999.

ix "The project manager pointed out": W. Wayt Gibbs, "Command and Control: Inside a hollowed-out mountain, software fiascoes—and a signal success," *Scientific American*, August 1997, pp. 33–34.

x "In contrast, the average": For data on risk management, see Capers Jones, *Assessment and Control of Software Risks*, Englewood Cliffs, NJ: Yourdon Press, 1994; and Andy Cole, "Runaway Projects—Cause and Effects," *Software World*, vol. 26, no. 3: pp. 3–5.

x "In contrast, the average": For a discussion of schedule overruns, see The Standish Group, "Charting the Seas of Information Technology," Dennis, MA: The Standish Group, 1994.

x "It attained an average": James Herbsleb, et al., *Benefits of CMM Based Software Process Improvement: Initial Results*. Pittsburgh: Software Engineering Institute, Document number CMU/SEI-94-TR-13, August 1994.

x "In the worst organizations": Capers Jones, *Patterns of Software Systems Failure and Success*. Boston, MA: International Thomson Computer Press, 1996.

x "An organization that committed": James Herbsleb, et al., *Benefits of CMM-Based Software Process Improvement: Initial Results*. Pittsburgh: Software Engineering Institute, Document number CMU/SEI-94-TR-13, August 1994.

x "Problems with the baggage": Robert L. Glass, *Software Runaways*. Englewood Cliffs, NJ: Prentice Hall, 1998; W. Wayt Gibbs, "Software's Chronic Crisis," *Scientific American*, September 1994, pp. 86–95.

x "The FAA's Advanced Automation System": Robert N. Britcher, "Why (some) large computer projects fail," in Robert L. Glass, *Software Runaways*. Englewood Cliffs, NJ: Prentice Hall, 1998; and W. Wayt Gibbs, "Software's Chronic Crisis," *Scientific American*, September 1994, pp. 86–95.

x "The IRS bumbled": Gary H. Anthes, "IRS Project Failures Cost Taxpayers $50B Annually," *Computerworld*, 14 October 1996.

Page

x "After topping $44 million": Chuck Appleby, "Agency's Drive to Nowhere," *InformationWeek*, 13 June 1994.

x "The B-2 bomber": Charles Fishman, "They Write the Right Stuff," *Fast Company*, December 1996.

x "The Ariane 5 rocket": Bashar Nuseibeh, "Ariane 5: Who Dunnit?" *IEEE Software*, May/June 1997, pp. 15–16.

x "The state of Washington": Peter G. Neumann, *Computer Related Risks*. Reading, MA: Addison-Wesley, 1995.

x "The project lead of Lotus": Lauren Ruth Wiener, *Digital Woes: Why We Should Not Depend on Software*. Reading, MA: Addison-Wesley, 1993.

xii "Industry researchers have long": Harlan D. Mills, *Software Productivity*. Boston, MA: Little, Brown, 1983.

xiii "More recently, researchers": Edward Yourdon, *Rise and Resurrection of the American Programmer*. Englewood Cliffs, NJ: Prentice Hall, 1996.

Chapter 1: Software Dinosaurs

Page

3 "In 1975, Fred Brooks compared": Frederick P. Brooks, Jr., *The Mythical Man-Month, Anniversary Edition*. Reading, MA: Addison-Wesley, 1995. The original edition was published in 1975.

4 "According to some estimates": Data on frequency of schedule pressure comes from Capers Jones, *Assessment and Control of Software Risks*. Englewood Cliffs, NJ: Yourdon Press, 1994. For information on common schedule performance, see The Standish Group, "Charting the Seas of Information Technology," Dennis, MA: The Standish Group, 1994; and Capers Jones, *Patterns of Software Systems Failure and Success*. Boston: International Thomson Computer Press, 1996.

4 "Overtime is more the norm": Discussed in detail in Steve McConnell, *Rapid Development*. Redmond, WA: Microsoft Press, 1996.

4 "As far back as the mid-1960s": Gene Bylinsky, "Help Wanted: 50,000 Programmers," *Fortune*, March 1967, pp. 141 ff.

4 "In 1975, Fred Brooks pointed": Frederick P. Brooks, Jr., *The Mythical Man-Month*. Reading, MA: Addison-Wesley, 1975.

4 "Many people today complain": *IEEE Software*, May/June 1999.

4 "Thirty years ago, total employment": Gene Bylinsky, "Help Wanted: 50,000 Programmers," *Fortune*, March 1967, pp. 141 ff.

4 "The initial Windows NT project": This number is an estimate. It is based on the reported cost for Microsoft Windows NT being $150 million (Pascal Zachary, *Showstopper! The Breakneck Race to Create Windows NT and the Next Generation at Microsoft*. New York: Free Press, 1994) and a fully burdened labor cost of $100,000/staff year.

4 "The initial Windows NT project": Effort was approximately 5,000 staff months. Frederick P. Brooks, Jr., *The Mythical Man-Month*. Reading, MA: Addison-Wesley, 1975.

4 "Recent surveys have found": Andy Cole, "Runaway Projects—Cause and Effects," *Software World*, vol. 26, no. 3, pp. 3–5; The Standish Group, "Charting the Seas of Information Technology," Dennis, MA: The Standish Group, 1994.

4 "But requirements problems are": Robert A. Frosch, "A New Look at Systems Engineering," *IEEE Spectrum*, September 1969.

Page

5 "From time to time we still": Charles Rich and Richard C. Waters, "Automatic Programming: Myths and Prospects," *IEEE Computer*, August 1988.

5 "But this conjecture was": Gene Bylinsky, "Help Wanted: 50,000 Programmers," *Fortune*, March 1967, pp. 141 ff.

Chapter 2: Fool's Gold

Page

11 "About 75 percent of software": This average is based on the number of software projects at SW-CMM Level 1. See Chapter 7 for more details about this statistic.

11 "Several studies have found that": Software Engineering Institute, quoted in Charles Fishman, "They Write the Right Stuff," *Fast Company*, December 1996; Harlan D. Mills, *Software Productivity*. Boston, MA: Little, Brown, 1983, pp. 71–81; David Wheeler, Bill Brykczynski, and Reginald Meeson, *Software Inspection: An Industry Best Practice*. Los Alamitos, CA: IEEE Computer Society Press, 1996; Capers Jones, *Programming Productivity*. New York: McGraw-Hill, 1986; Barry W. Boehm, "Improving Software Productivity," *IEEE Computer*, September 1987, pp. 43–57.

12 "Figure 2-4": Steve McConnell, *Software Project Survival Guide*. Redmond, WA: Microsoft Press, 1997. *Software Project Survival Guide* contains a more in-depth description of these dynamics.

12 "This gloomy picture is no": The Standish Group, "Charting the Seas of Information Technology," Dennis, MA: The Standish Group, 1994; Capers Jones, *Assessment and Control of Software Risks*. Englewood Cliffs, NJ: Yourdon Press, 1994.

12 "The reason the project is canceled": Capers Jones, *Assessment and Control of Software Risks*. Englewood Cliffs, NJ: Yourdon Press, 1994.

14 "Figure 2-5": The "advanced project" profile is based on projects performed by NASA's Software Engineering Lab. The "typical project" is from project data I've compiled from my consulting work and is consistent with data reported by Capers Jones, *Patterns of Software Systems Failure and Success*. Boston: International Thomson Computer Press, 1996, and other sources.

16 "Projects that focused on achieving": Capers Jones, *Programming Productivity*. New York: McGraw-Hill, 1986.

16 "Figure 2-7": Capers Jones, *Applied Software Measurement: Assuring Productivity and Quality*, 2d ed. New York: McGraw-Hill, 1997.

17 "Technologies and methodologies": Frederick P. Brooks, Jr., "No Silver Bullets—Essence and Accidents of Software Engineering," *Computer*, April 1987, pp. 10–19.

18 "The elephant analogy is more apt": Robert L. Glass, *Software Runaways*, Englewood Cliffs, NJ: Prentice Hall, 1998.

19 "Several studies have found that": J. Vosburgh, B. Curtis, R. Wolverton, B. Albert, H. Malec, S. Hoben, and Y. Liu, "Productivity Factors and Programming Environments," *Proceedings of the 7th International Conference on Software Engineering*, Los Alamitos, CA: IEEE Computer Society, 1984, pp. 143–152; Albert L. Lederer, and Jayesh Prasad, "Nine Management Guidelines for Better Cost Estimating," *Communications of the ACM*, February 1992, pp. 51–59; The Standish Group, "Charting the Seas of Information Technology," Dennis, MA: The Standish Group, 1994; Capers Jones, *Assessment and Control of Software Risks*, Englewood Cliffs, NJ: Yourdon Press, 1994.

19 "They are also a major factor": Capers Jones, *Assessment and Control of Software Risks*, Englewood Cliffs, NJ: Yourdon Press, 1994.

Chapter 3: Orphans Preferred

Page

23 "We realize the skills": *Seattle Times*, October 8, 1995. Emphasis in original.

24 "*USA Today* reported that": Del Jones, "Stereotype turns students off of high-paying career," *USA Today*, 16 February 1998, pp. 1B–2B.

24 "The *Wall Street Journal*": Po Bronson, "Manager's Journal," *Wall Street Journal*, 9 February 1998.

24 "The associate director of": Amy Harmon, "Software Jobs Go Begging," *New York Times*, 13 January 1998, p. A1.

25 "Two large studies have found": Rob Thomsett, "Effective Project Teams: A Dilemma, A Model, A Solution," *American Programmer*, July/August 1990, pp. 25–35; Michael L. Lyons, "The DP Psyche," *Datamation*, 15 August 1985, pp. 103–109.

25 "*ISTJs* comprise 25–40": Rob Thomsett, "Effective Project Teams: A Dilemma, A Model, A Solution," *American Programmer*, July/August 1990, pp. 25–35; Michael L. Lyons, "The DP Psyche," *Datamation*, 15 August 1985, pp. 103–109; R. P. Bostrom and K. M. Kaiser, "Personality Differences within Systems Project Teams," *Proceedings of the 18th Annual Computer Personnel Research Conference*, ACM No. 443810, 1981.

25 "Programmers are indeed": Rob Thomsett, "Effective Project Teams: A Dilemma, A Model, A Solution," *American Programmer*, July/August 1990, pp. 25–35; Michael L. Lyons, "The DP Psyche," *Datamation*, 15 August 1985, pp. 103–109.

25 "About 60 percent of software": *1996 Digest of Education Statistics*. Washington, DC: National Center for Education Statistics, Document number NCES 96-133, 1996. Data is from "Table 8.— Years of school completed by persons age 25 and over and 25 to 29, by race and sex: 1910 to 1995."

25 "Eighty to ninety percent of software": Rob Thomsett, "Effective Project Teams: A Dilemma, A Model, A Solution," *American Programmer*, July/August 1990, pp. 25–35; Michael L. Lyons, "The DP Psyche," *Datamation*, 15 August 1985, pp. 103–109; R. P. Bostrom and K. M. Kaiser, "Personality Differences within Systems Project Teams," *Proceedings of the 18th Annual Computer Personnel Research Conference*, ACM No. 443810, 1981.

26 "One study of designers": Robert L. Glass, *Software Creativity*. Englewood Cliffs, NJ: Prentice Hall PTR, 1994.

28 "If private dreams are nursed": Pascal Zachary, *Showstopper! The Breakneck Race to Create Windows NT and the Next Generation at Microsoft*. New York: Free Press, 1994.

28 "The average project spends": Software Engineering Institute, quoted in Charles Fishman, "They Write the Right Stuff," *Fast Company*, December 1996; Harlan D. Mills, *Software Productivity*. Boston, MA: Little, Brown, 1983, pp. 71–81; David Wheeler, Bill Brykczynski, and Reginald Meeson, *Software Inspection: An Industry Best Practice*. Los Alamitos, CA: IEEE Computer Society Press, 1996; Capers Jones, *Programming Productivity*. New York: McGraw-Hill, 1986; Barry W. Boehm, "Improving Software Productivity," *IEEE Computer*, September 1987, pp. 43–57.

29 "As an example of loyalty": See, for example, R.M. Stallman, "The GNU Manifesto," 1985, http://www.fsf.org/gnu/manifesto.html; E. S. Raymond, "Homesteading the Noosphere," 1998, http://www.earthspace.net/~esr/writings/homesteading/.

30 "Figure 3-1": Bill Lowell and Angela Burgess, "A Moving Target: Studies Try to Define the IT Workforce," *IT Professional*, May/June 1999.

Page

30 "The majority of software": The data used to create this graph is from "Table 253.—Bachelor's, master's, and doctor's degrees conferred by institutions of higher education, by sex of student and field of study: 1995–96," *1998 Digest of Education Statistics*. Washington, DC: National Center for Education Statistics, Document number NCES 1999036, 4 May 1999.

30 "In high school, only 17": Amy Harmon, "Software Jobs Go Begging," *New York Times*, 13 January 1998, p. A1.

31 "According to the United Engineering": Bill Lowell and Angela Burgess, "A Moving Target: Studies Try to Define the IT Workforce," *IT Professional*, May/June 1999.

31 "Universities in the United": *1996 Digest of Education Statistics*. Washington, DC: National Center for Education Statistics, Document number NCES 96-133, 1996.

31 "Table 3-1": *1998-99 Occupational Outlook Handbook*. Washington, DC: Bureau of Labor Statistics, 1999.

32 "Table 3-2": These numbers are projections for the year 2000 based on actual employment data for 1996 and projected annual increases contained in "Occupational projections to 2006," *Monthly Labor Review*, November 1997.

33 "Table 3-3": Capers Jones, *Applied Software Measurement: Assuring Productivity and Quality*, 2d ed. New York: McGraw-Hill, 1997.

33 "This labor shortage has been": Gene Bylinsky, "Help Wanted: 50,000 programmers," *Fortune*, March 1967, pp. 141 ff.

33 "Software-related jobs are rated": Les Krantz, *Jobs Rated Almanac*. New York: St. Martins Press, 1999.

33 "Project managers both love": James Bach, "Enough About Process: What We Need Are Heroes," *IEEE Software*, March 1995, pp. 96–98.

34 "A study at IBM found": Gerald M. McCue, "IBM's Santa Teresa Laboratory—Architectural Design for Program Development," *IBM Systems Journal*, vol. 17, no. 1, 1978, pp. 4–25.

34 "Another study of 31 software": B. Lakhanpal, "Understanding the Factors Influencing the Performance of Software Development Groups: An Exploratory Group-Level Analysis," *Information and Software Technology*, 35 (8), 1993, pp. 468–473.

Chapter 4: Software Engineering Is Not Computer Science

Page

38 "The distinction between science": For much of this discussion, I am indebted to David L. Parnas, especially for his paper, "Software Engineering Programmes are not Computer Science Programmes," *IEEE Software*, November/December 1999.

40 "As David Parnas points out": David L. Parnas, "Software Engineering: An Unconsummated Marriage," *Software Engineering Notes*, November 1997.

41 "Some engineering companies report": Robin Baines, "Across Disciplines: Risk, Design, Method, Process, and Tools," *IEEE Software*, July/August 1998, pp. 61–64.

Chapter 5: After the Gold Rush

Page

50 "Post–gold rush customers": Geoffrey Moore, *Crossing the Chasm*. New York: Harper Business, 1991.

52 "Larry Constantine describes": Larry Constantine, "Under Pressure," *Software Development*, October 1995, pp. 111–12.

52 "They reappeared a few months": Larry Constantine, "Re: Architecture," *Software Development*, January 1996, pp. 87–88.

52 "This general value of applying": James Herbsleb, et al., "Software Quality and the Capability Maturity Model," *Communications of the ACM*, June 1997, pp. 30–40.

Chapter 6: Engineering a Profession

Page

56 "Although we take the safety": Samuel C. Florman, *The Existential Pleasures of Engineering*, 2d ed. 1994, New York: St. Martin's Griffin, 1994.

56 "In Canada, engineering folklore": I call this story "folklore" because several Canadian professional engineers have independently told me that the iron in the iron ring traditionally is thought to come from the wreckage of the iron bridge that collapsed in Quebec City in 1907. Published information about the Canadian iron ring ceremony contains no mention of the Quebec City bridge. However, the actual ceremony is secret, so it might contain mention of this bridge.

56 "Any reader of the *Forum*": Digest subscription to this forum is available by e-mailing risks-request@csl.sri.com or on Usenet at comp.risks.

56 "The parking software didn't": All the examples in this paragraph come from Peter G. Neumann, *Computer Related Risks*. Reading, MA: Addison-Wesley, 1995.

59 "Figure 6-3": Mary Shaw, "Prospects for an Engineering Discipline of Software," *IEEE Software*, November 1990, pp. 15 f.

61 "The airfoil wing section": Christopher Alexander, quoted in Robert L. Glass, *Software Creativity*. Englewood Cliffs, NJ: Prentice Hall PTR, 1994.

61 "In fact it isn't even considered": Herbert Simon, *The Sciences of the Artificial*. Cambridge, MA: MIT Press, 1969.

62 "Following is a short list of": For more information, see Capers Jones, *Assessment and Control of Software Risks*. Englewood Cliffs, NJ: Yourdon Press, 1994.

62 "In *The Structure of Scientific*": Thomas S. Kuhn, *The Structure of Scientific Revolutions*, 2nd ed. Chicago: The University of Chicago Press, 1970.

Chapter 7: Ptolemaic Reasoning

Page

66 "The SW-CMM classifies": The single best description of the SW-CMM is Carnegie Mellon University/Software Engineering Institute, *The Capability Maturity Model: Guidelines for Improving the Software Process*. Reading, MA: Addison-Wesley, 1995. Other documents are available for download from the SEI's web site at http://www.sei.cmu.edu/.

67 "The underlying principle of": M. E. Conway, "How Do Committees Invent?" *Datamation*, vol. 14, no. 4, 1968, pp. 27–31.

Page

68 "Figure 7-1": SEI, "Process Maturity Profile of the Software Community 1998 Year End Update," Software Engineering Institute, March 1999.

68 "Figure 7-2": SEI, "Process Maturity Profile of the Software Community 1998 Year End Update," Software Engineering Institute, March 1999.

69 "The trend shown by these": This trend is confirmed by Capers Jones, *Patterns of Software Systems Failure and Success*. Boston: International Thomson Computer Press, 1996.

69 "An in-depth study of 13": James Herbsleb, et al., *Benefits of CMM Based Software Process Improvement: Initial Results*. Pittsburgh: Software Engineering Institute, Document number CMU/SEI-94-TR-13, August 1994.

69 "Table 7-1": Data in this table is from James Herbsleb, et al., *Benefits of CMM Based Software Process Improvement: Initial Results*. Pittsburgh: Software Engineering Institute, Document number CMU/SEI-94-TR-13, August 1994.

70 "As Figure 7-3 shows": SEI, "Process Maturity Profile of the Software Community 1998 Year End Update," Software Engineering Institute, March 1999.

70 "Figure 7-3": SEI, "Process Maturity Profile of the Software Community 1998 Year End Update," Software Engineering Institute, March 1999.

71 "My Ptolemaic seminar attendee": Tom DeMarco and Timothy Lister, *Peopleware: Productive Projects and Teams,* 2d ed. New York: Dorset House, 1999.

71 "In Level 3 organizations": James Herbsleb, et al., "Software Quality and the Capability Maturity Model," *Communications of the ACM*, June 1997, pp. 30–40.

71 "This relationship between process": W. Wayt Gibbs, "Command and Control: Inside a hollowed-out mountain, software fiascoes—and a signal success," *Scientific American*, August 1997, pp. 33–34; Buford D. Tackett III and Buddy Van Doren, "Process Control for Error Free Software: A Software Success Story," *IEEE Software*, May 1999; and Richard L. Randall, et al., "Product-Line Reuse Delivers a System for One-Fifth the Cost in One-Half the Time," *Crosstalk*, August 1996.

72 "In a survey of about 50": James Herbsleb, et al., "Software Quality and the Capability Maturity Model," *Communications of the ACM*, June 1997, pp. 30–40.

72 "A survey at Ogden Air": Leon G. Oldham, et al., "Benefits Realized from Climbing the CMM Ladder," *Crosstalk*, May 1999.

73 "The on-board shuttle software": Charles Fishman, "They Write the Right Stuff," *Fast Company*, December 1996.

73 "A Standish Group survey": The Standish Group, "Charting the Seas of Information Technology," Dennis, MA: The Standish Group, 1994.

73 "The level of estimation error": See, for example, Capers Jones, *Patterns of Software Systems Failure and Success*. Boston, MA: International Thomson Computer Press, 1996.

74 "Figure 7-4": Dr. Patricia K. Lawlis, Capt. Robert M. Flowe, and Capt. James B. Thordahl, "A Correlational Study of the CMM and Software Development Performance," *Crosstalk,* September 1995.

75 "Organizations that do systematic": See, for example, University of Southern California, *Cocomo II Model Definition Manual, version 1.4*, n.d. (circa 1997), which uses 2.45 as its baseline coefficient and 1.15 as the nominal exponent.

75 "The SEL uses the": NASA Software Engineering Laboratory, *Software Engineering Laboratory (SEL) Relationships, Models, and Management Rules*. Greenbelt, MD: Goddard Space Flight Center, NASA, Document number SEL-91-001, 1991.

Page

76 "Seventy-seven percent of": James Herbsleb, et al., "Software Quality and the Capability Maturity Model," *Communications of the ACM*, June 1997, pp. 30–40. An "outlier" is a value that is more than 1.5 box lengths greater than the 75th percentile or more than 1.5 box lengths less than the 25th percentile.

77 "JCAHO lists these reasons": See the JCAHO web site at http://jcaho.org/.

Chapter 8: Body of Knowledge

Page

79 "A person needs to know": Mary Shaw, "Prospects for an Engineering Discipline of Software," *IEEE Software*, November 1990, pp. 15f.

80 "In 1987, Fred Brooks published": Frederick P. Brooks, Jr., "No Silver Bullets—Essence and Accidents of Software Engineering," *Computer*, April 1987, pp. 10–19.

82 "Consider that the first fully": Donald Knuth, *The Art of Computer Programming, Volume 3, Sorting and Searching.* Reading, MA: Addison-Wesley, 1973, p. 419.

82 "C. Böhm and G. Jacopini published": C. Böhm and G. Jacopini, "Flow Diagrams, Turing Machines, and Languages with Only Two Formation Rules," *Communications of the ACM*, May 1966, pp. 366–71.

82 "Edsger Dijkstra wrote his famous": Edsger Dijkstra, *Communications of the ACM*, vol. 11, 1968, pp. 147–148.

82 "Larry Constantine, Glenford Myers": Larry Constantine, Glenford Myers, and Wayne Stevens, "Structured Design," *IBM Systems Journal*, No. 2, 1974, pp. 115–39.

82 "Tom Gilb published the first": Tom Gilb, *Software Metrics*, Cambridge, MA: Winthrop Publishers, 1977.

82 "Tom DeMarco published the first": Tom DeMarco, *Structured Analysis and System Specification.* Englewood Cliffs, NJ: Prentice Hall, 1979.

82 "Researchers at Université": Additional information is available on the Swebok web site at http://www.swebok.org/.

84 "Project leaders should still": W. R. Duncan, "A Guide to the Project Management Body of Knowledge," Newtown Square, PA: Project Management Institute, 1996.

85 "Figure 8-3": Pierre Bourque, et al., "Guide to the Software Engineering Body of Knowledge: A Strawman Version," Université du Québec à Montréal, September 1998.

86 "Figure 8-4": Leonard Tripp, "Professionalism of Software Engineering: Next Steps," Keynote address at *12th Conference on Software Engineering Education and Training*, 22 March 1999.

Chapter 9: Novum Organum

Page

92 "According to legal precedents": Adapted from Cem Kaner, "Computer Malpractice," *Software QA*, vol. 3, no. 4, 1997, p. 23.

92 "Gary Ford and Norman E. Gibbs": Gary Ford and Norman E. Gibbs, "A Mature Profession of Software Engineering," SEI, CMU, Document number CMU/SEI-96-TR-004, January 1996.

96 "Table 9-1": Adapted from Gary Ford and Norman E. Gibbs, "A Mature Profession of Software Engineering," SEI, CMU, Document number CMU/SEI-96-TR-004, January 1996.

Chapter 10: Stinking Badges

Page

102 "The American Society for": Cem Kaner, "Computer Malpractice," *Software QA*, vol. 3, no. 4, 1997, p. 23.

103 "The following list gives": Gary Ford and Norman E. Gibbs, "A Mature Profession of Software Engineering," SEI, CMU, Document number CMU/SEI-96-TR-004, January 1996.

104 "Table 10-1": Gary Ford and Norman E. Gibbs, "A Mature Profession of Software Engineering," SEI, CMU, Document number CMU/SEI-96-TR-004, January 1996.

104 "We produce some safety-critical": Ford and Gibbs make a similar point—they estimate that less than 10 percent of software workers will receive licenses. Gary Ford and Norman E. Gibbs, "A Mature Profession of Software Engineering," SEI, CMU, Document number CMU/SEI-96-TR-004, January 1996.

104 "The movement to license": Texas Board of Professional Engineers' web site, http://www.main.org/peboard/.

104 "The ACM and IEEE Computer": Software Engineering Coordinating Committee web site, http://www.computer.org/tab/swecc/.

105 "Texas's approval clears": Association of Professional Engineers and Geoscientists of British Columbia, "Professional Engineers and Geoscientists to Register Software Professional Engineers," 25 June 1999 (press release).

106 "Courts in the United States": Cem Kaner, "Computer Malpractice," *Software QA*, vol. 3, no. 4, 1997, p. 23.

107 "As Fred Brooks pointed out": Frederick P. Brooks, Jr., *The Mythical Man-Month, Anniversary Edition*. Reading, MA: Addison-Wesley, 1995.

108 "I predict that we'll see": Harlan D. Mills, *Software Productivity*. Boston, MA: Little, Brown, 1983, pp. 71–81.

108 "In British Columbia, the current": Tom Calvert, "Computer and Software Engineering Task Force White Paper," 16 March 1999. Available from APEGBC's web site at http://www.apeg.bc.ca.

112 "In Canada, engineers who graduate": You can find a description of the iron ring ceremony at http://www.ironring.ca.

Chapter 11: Architects and Carpenters

Page

114 "Table 11-1 summarizes": The McMaster curriculum can be accessed via the Internet at http://www.cas.mcmaster.ca/cas/undergraduate/. The RIT program can be accessed at http://www.rit.edu/~930www/Proj/UGrad/UGradCat/colleges/cast/.

118 "In the United States": This data is from "Table 376.—Total annual money income and median income of persons 25 years old and over, by educational attainment and sex: 1994," *1996 Digest of Education Statistics*, Washington, DC: National Center for Education Statistics, Document number NCES 96-133, 1996.

118 "The Bureau of Labor Statistics": Bureau of Labor Statistics, *1998 Occupational Outlook Handbook*, Washington, DC, 1988.

120 "Capers Jones estimates that": Capers Jones, *Assessment and Control of Software Risks*. Englewood Cliffs, NJ: Yourdon Press, 1994.

Page

120 "One chief programmer": Frederick P. Brooks, Jr., *The Mythical Man-Month, Anniversary Edition*. Reading, MA: Addison-Wesley, 1995.

120 "A test project in the": F. Terry Baker, "Chief Programmer Team Management of Production Programming," *IBM Systems Journal*, vol. 11, no. 1, 1972, pp. 56–73; F. Terry Baker and Harlan D. Mills, "Chief Programmer Teams," *Datamation*, vol. 19, no. 12, December 1973, pp. 58–61.

120 "Studies about other software": Fred Brooks makes a similar point in the 20th Anniversary Edition of the *Mythical Man-Month*, though he doesn't relate it back to the surgical team: "I came to insist that student teams as small as four people choose a manager and a separate architect. Defining distinct roles in such small teams may be a little extreme, but I have observed it to work well and to contribute to design success even for small teams."

122 "Table 11-2": Adapted from Capers Jones, *Assessment and Control of Software Risks*. Englewood Cliffs, NJ: Yourdon Press, 1994; and Capers Jones, *Patterns of Software Systems Failure and Success*. Boston: International Thomson Computer Press, 1996.

Chapter 12: Hard Knocks

Page

126 "Capers Jones points out": Capers Jones, "Gaps in Programming Education," *IEEE Computer*, April 1995, pp. 70–71.

126 "The Boeing Company": Gary Ford and Norman E. Gibbs, "A Mature Profession of Software Engineering," SEI, CMU, Document number CMU/SEI-96-TR-004, January 1996.

127 "Figure 12-1": The data used to create this graph is from "Table 250.— Bachelor's degrees conferred by institutions of higher education, by discipline division: 1970–71 to 1995–96," *1998 Digest of Education Statistics*, Washington, DC: National Center for Education Statistics, Document number NCES 1999036, 4 May 1999.

127 "The conventional explanation": Del Jones, "Stereotype turns students off of high-paying career," *USA Today*, 16 February 1998, pp. 1B–2B; Amy Harmon, "Software Jobs Go Begging," *New York Times*, 13 January 1998, p. A1.

129 "A handful are offered": For current information, see my company's web site at http://www.construx.com/profession/.

129 "In Canada, bachelor's": The United States and Canada may have additional programs that I have overlooked. The programs listed are the programs I knew about at the time the book was published.

129 "Several other North American": Programs are being considered at Monmouth University, Georgia Tech, and San Jose State University, among others.

131 "During the mid-1900s": Gary Ford and Norman E. Gibbs, "A Mature Profession of Software Engineering," SEI, CMU, Document number CMU/SEI-96-TR-004, January 1996.

131 "The CSAB criteria for": "Criteria For Accrediting Programs In Computer Science In The United States," Computer Science Accreditation Commission of the Computer Science Accreditation Board, June 1996.

132 "In contrast, the ABET": "Criteria for Accrediting Engineering Programs," Accreditation Board for Engineering and Technology, Inc., 1 November 1998.

132 "In Washington state": "Washington Society of Certified Public Accountants," http://www.wscpa.org/.

132 "Engineers in Washington": "Continuing Education Workshop," *The Washington Board Journal*, Winter/Spring 1999, p. 10.

Chapter 13: The Professional's Code

Page

136 "A code of ethics establishes": See, for example, the American Institute of Architects' *Code of Ethics and Professional Conduct* at http://www.aiaonline.com/professional/; the American Institute for Certified Public Accountants' *Code of Professional Conduct* at http://www.aicpa.org/; the National Society of Professional Engineers' *Code of Ethics for Engineers* at http://www.nspe.org/; the American Society of Mechanical Engineers' *Code of Ethics of Engineers* at http://www.asme.org/; and the Institute of Electrical and Electronics Engineers' *Code of Ethics* at http://www.ieee.org/. Current links for each of these codes of ethics are available from my company's web site at http://www.construx.com/profession/.

136 "Other engineering codes": See, for example, the National Society of Professional Engineers' *Code of Ethics for Engineers* at http://www.nspe.org/.

140 "One publisher reported that": Reported in Tom DeMarco and Timothy Lister, *Peopleware: Productive Projects and Teams*, 2d ed. New York: Dorset House, 1999.

Chapter 14: Alchemy

Page

143 "Q: What are the most exciting/promising": "ACM Fellow Profile: David Lorge Parnas," *ACM Software Engineering Notes*, May 1999, pp. 10–14.

144 "Table 14-1": For more information about these best practices, see Steve McConnell, *Rapid Development*. Redmond, WA: Microsoft Press, 1996.

144 "Automated estimation tools": Capers Jones, *Assessment and Control of Software Risks*. Englewood Cliffs, NJ: Yourdon Press, 1994.

144 "Evolutionary delivery": Tom Gilb, *Principles of Software Engineering Management*. Wokingham, England: Addison-Wesley, 1988.

144 "Measurement": Tom Gilb, *Software Metrics*. Cambridge, MA: Winthrop Publishers, 1977.

144 "Productivity environments": Barry W. Boehm, et al., "A Software Development Environment for Improving Productivity," *IEEE Computer*, June 1984, pp. 30–44; Tom DeMarco and Timothy Lister, "Programmer Performance and the Effects of the Workplace," in *Proceedings of the 8th International Conference on Software Engineering*, August 1985, pp. 268–72.

144 "Risk management planning": Risk management is much older than software, but software-specific papers on risk management began appearing with F. W. McFarlan, "Portfolio Approach to Information Systems," *Harvard Business Review*, September/October 1981, pp. 142–50.

144 "Change board": Change control boards are much older than software, but software-specific books and papers on software change control boards (or, more generally, on software configuration management) began appearing with Edward H. Bersoff, *Proceedings of the Software Quality and Assurance Workshop*, a joint publication of ACM *Performance Evaluation Review*, vol. 7, nos. 3 and 4; and ACM *Software Engineering Notes*, vol. 3, no. 5, 1978.

144 "Throwaway user-interface prototyping": Frederick P. Brooks, Jr., *The Mythical Man-Month*. Reading, MA: Addison-Wesley, 1975.

144 "JAD sessions": JAD sessions were used at IBM as early as 1977, but were first reported in print in Gary Rush, "The Fast Way to Define System Requirements," *Computerworld*, 7 October 1985.

Page

144 "Information hiding": David L. Parnas, "On the Criteria to Be Used in Decomposing Systems into Modules," *Communications of the ACM,* vol. 5, no. 12, December 1972, pp. 1053–58.

144 "Design for change": David L. Parnas, "Designing Software for Ease of Extension and Contraction," *IEEE Transactions on Software Engineering,* vol. SE-5, March 1979, pp. 128–138.

144 "Source-code control": Various source-code control tools have been around since before 1980, but an early reference in print is Edward H. Bersoff, et al., *Software Configuration Management.* Englewood Cliffs, NJ: Prentice Hall, 1980.

144 "Incremental integration": Glenford J. Myers, *The Art of Software Testing.* New York: John Wiley and Sons, 1979.

145 "Branch-coverage testing": Glenford J. Myers, *The Art of Software Testing.* New York: John Wiley and Sons, 1979.

145 "Inspections": M. E. Fagan, "Design and Code Inspections to Reduce Errors in Program Development," *IBM Systems Journal,* vol. 15, no. 3, 1976, pp. 182–211.

145 "Software Engineering Institute's": W. S. Humphrey and W. L. Sweet, *A Method for Assessing the Software Engineering Capability of Contractors.* Pittsburgh: Software Engineering Institute, Report CMU/SEI-87-TR-23, 1987.

145 "Software Engineering Process Groups": Watts S. Humphrey, *Managing the Software Process.* Reading, MA: Addison-Wesley, 1989.

145 "Researchers have found": Mary Shaw, "Prospects for an Engineering Discipline of Software," *IEEE Software,* November 1990, pp. 15f; Sridhar A. Raghavan and Donald R. Chand, "Diffusing Software-Engineering Methods," *IEEE Software,* July 1989, pp. 81–90.

145 "The seminal work on": Everett M. Rogers, *Diffusion of Innovations,* 4th ed. New York: The Free Press, 1995.

146 "Figure 14-1": Everett M. Rogers, *Diffusion of Innovations,* 4th ed. New York: The Free Press, 1995.

146 "Rogers' work was extended": Geoffrey Moore, *Crossing the Chasm.* New York: Harper Business, 1991.

147 "Figure 14-2": Geoffrey Moore, *Crossing the Chasm.* New York: Harper Business, 1991.

147 "When presented with an": Sridhar A. Raghavan and Donald R. Chand, "Diffusing Software-Engineering Methods," *IEEE Software,* July 1989, pp. 81–90.

151 "As one author said": J.D. Eveland, quoted in Everett M. Rogers, *Diffusion of Innovations,* 4th ed. New York: The Free Press, 1995. The details in this discussion about agricultural innovation are all drawn from Rogers' book.

152 "One of the best organizations": Sharon R. Waligora, Linda C. Landis, and Jerry T. Doland, "Closing the Loop on Improvement: Packaging Experience in the Software Engineering Laboratory," *Proceedings of the Nineteenth Annual Software Engineering Workshop, November 30–December 1, 1994,* NASA Goddard Space Flight Center, Greenbelt, MD, Document number SEL-94-006.

152 "The SEI was created": See the SEI's web site at http://www.sei.cmu.edu/.

152 "At about 300 employees": Agricultural worker statistics are from "Table 2, Employment by occupation, 1996 and projected 2006," in "Occupational projections to 2006," *Monthly Labor Review,* November 1997.

152 "Not surprisingly, the industries": Will Hayes and Dave Zubrow, *Moving On Up: Data and Experience Doing CMM-Based Process Improvement.* Pittsburgh: Software Engineering Institute, Document number CMU/SEI-95-TR-008, August 1995.

Page

153 "Ed Yourdon explained": Edward Yourdon and Larry L. Constantine, *Structured Design: Fundamentals of a Discipline of Computer Program and Systems Design*. Englewood Cliffs, NJ: Yourdon Press, 1979.

153 "It wasn't until Meilir": Meilir Page-Jones, *The Practical Guide to Structured Systems Design*. Englewood Cliffs, NJ: Yourdon Press, 1988.

153 "It wasn't until Meilir": Larry L. Constantine, *Constantine on Peopleware*. Englewood Cliffs, NJ: Yourdon Press, 1995.

INDEX

Note: page numbers in italics refer to illustrations.

Association for Computing Machinery.
　　See ACM (Association for Computing
　　Machinery)
Association of Professional Engineers and
　　Geoscientists of British Columbia
　　(APEGBC), 105, 108–9
ATAMS project (Cheyenne Mountain), 71,
　　73
Australia
　　Australian Computer Society Software
　　　Challenge, 52
　　undergraduate degrees in software
　　　engineering, 129

B

Bacon, Francis, 89–90, 97
bidding for projects. *See* costs
Boeing Company, education and, 126
Brooks, Fred, 3–4, 80–81, 120
budgets. *See* costs
bureaucracy, organizational improvement
　　and, 71, 72, 73
buzzwords. *See* silver bullets

C

Canada
　　Canadian Engineering Accreditation
　　　Board, 132
　　undergraduate degrees in software
　　　engineering, 129
careers. *See* employment
CASE tools as silver bullet innovation, 17
certification. *See also* accreditation;
　　licensing
　　in development of professions, 93–94,
　　　93, 95, 102
　　in development of software engineering
　　　profession, *96*

certification, *continued*
　　of engineering technicians and
　　　technologists, 118
　　for software engineers, 102, 116, 120
Certified Computing Professional
　　designation, 102
Certified Network Engineer designation,
　　102
CFR (Code of Federal Regulations), 91–92
Cheyenne Mountain ATAMS project, 71,
　　73
code-and-fix development
　　in adoption sequence of diffusion, 148,
　　　149, 150–51
　　code of ethics for software development
　　　and, 140
　　cost of defect-correction, 11, 70
　　as flat-earth approach, 91
　　overview, 11–15
　　as Ptolemaic practice, 75
　　reasons for using, 11, *12,* 13, 42
　　SW-CMM levels and, 66–67
code of ethics
　　in development of professions, *93,* 94,
　　　135
　　in development of software engineering
　　　profession, *96*
　　for software development, 136–41
Code of Federal Regulations (CFR), 91–92
coding. *See* source code
cognitive sciences, software engineering
　　body of knowledge and, 85, *86*
commercial software development
　　evaluating and comparing contracting
　　　arrangements, 77
　　industry needs not met by current
　　　educational structure, 32, 40, 126–28
　　progress of, 152
　　science of software and, 61–62
　　specialists needed by companies, 121
　　as stage of discipline developing into
　　　engineering, 60

S

Steve McConnell

Steve McConnell is president and chief software engineer at Construx Software, where he divides his time between leading custom software projects, teaching classes, and writing books and articles. He is the author of the Microsoft Press books *Code Complete* (1993), *Rapid Development* (1996), and *Software Project Survival Guide* (1998). His books have twice won *Software Development* magazine's Jolt Excellence Award for outstanding software development book of the year. In 1998, readers of *Software Development* named Steve one of the three most influential people in the software industry along with Bill Gates and Linus Torvalds.

In his spare time, Steve serves as editor in chief of *IEEE Software* magazine. He is on the panel of experts that provides advice to the Software Engineering Body of Knowledge (SWEBOK) project, and is a member of IEEE and ACM.

Steve earned a bachelor's degree from Whitman College and a master's degree in software engineering from Seattle University. He lives in Bellevue, Washington with his wife, Tammy; daughter, Haley; and dog, Daisy.

If you have any comments or questions about this book, please contact Steve via e-mail at stevemcc@construx.com or via his web site at http://www.construx.com/stevemcc/.

Software Engineering Profession Web Site

`http://www.construx.com/profession/`

This book has a companion web site; the address is shown above. The web site contains materials related to the contents of this book, including professional reading lists, self-study plans, descriptions of current certification and licensing initiatives, links to university software engineering programs, and pointers to many other related web sites.

The manuscript for this book was prepared and submitted to Microsoft Press in electronic form. Text files were prepared using Microsoft Word 2000. Pages were composed by Microsoft Press using Adobe PageMaker 6.52 for Windows, with text and display type in Palatino. Composed pages were delivered to the printer as electronic prepress files.

Cover Designer
Greg Hickman

Cover Illustrator
Todd Daman

Interior Graphic Artist
Rob Nance

Principal Copy Editor
Cheryl Penner

Principal Compositor
Paula Gorelick

Best practices
for real-world software development

Now you can apply the industry's best software engineering practices to your own development projects with the BEST PRACTICES series from Microsoft Press. Written by some of the most knowledgeable and articulate practitioners in the business, these award-winning books take a pragmatic approach to managing the people, processes, and principles of software development. Use them to learn how to:

- Get high-pressure development schedules under control

- Energize software teams to work effectively
- Communicate delivery and quality expectations across the team and to management
- Keep costs down
- Deliver the best possible product to customers

Packed with practical, field-tested tools and tactics, BEST PRACTICES books offer candid accounts of what works and what doesn't, straight from the real-world experiences of the leading software vendors. Get them—and you get the inside track to everyday software excellence.

Code Complete	Debugging the Development Process	Dynamics of Software Development	Managing the Testing Process	Rapid Development	Writing Solid Code	Software Project Survival Guide
ISBN: 1-55615-484-4	ISBN: 1-55615-650-2	ISBN: 1-55615-823-8	ISBN: 0-7356-0584-X	ISBN: 1-55615-900-5	ISBN: 1-55615-551-4	ISBN: 1-57231-621-7
U.S.A. $35.00	U.S.A. $24.95	U.S.A. $24.95	U.S.A. $39.99	U.S.A. $35.00	U.S.A. $24.95	U.S.A. $24.99
UK £29.95	UK £22.99	UK £22.99	UK £37.49 [V.A.T. included]	UK £32.49	UK £22.99	UK £22.49
Canada $44.95	Canada $32.95	Canada $33.95	Canada $59.99	Canada $46.95	Canada $32.95	Canada $34.99

***Microsoft*®**

mspress.microsoft.com

Real-world developer training
for results on the job—and on the exam.

The Microsoft Certified Solution Developer (MCSD) credential is the premium certification for professionals who design and develop custom business solutions with Microsoft development tools, technologies, and platforms. Now you can build the skills and knowledge tested on the MCSD exams—and on the job—with these official Microsoft training kits.

Each MCSD TRAINING KIT features a comprehensive training manual, lab exercises, reusable source code, and sample exam questions. Work through the system of self-paced lessons and hands-on labs to gain practical experience with essential development tasks. By the end of the course you've created a full-featured working application—and you're ready for the corresponding exam!

Desktop Applications with Microsoft® Visual Basic® 6.0 MCSD Training Kit
ISBN: 0-7356-0620-X
U.S.A. $69.99
U.K.   £64.99 [V.A.T. included]
Canada $104.99

Desktop Applications with Microsoft Visual C++® 6.0 MCSD Training Kit
ISBN: 0-7356-0795-8
U.S.A. $69.99
U.K.   £64.99 [V.A.T. included]
Canada $104.99

Distributed Applications with Microsoft Visual Basic 6.0 MCSD Training Kit
ISBN: 0-7356-0833-4
U.S.A. $69.99
U.K.   £64.99 [V.A.T. included]
Canada $104.99

Analyzing Requirements and Defining Solution Architectures MCSD Training Kit
ISBN: 0-7356-0854-7
U.S.A. $69.99
U.K.   £64.99 [V.A.T. included]
Canada $104.99

Microsoft®
mspress.microsoft.com

After the Gold Rush: Creating a True Profession of Software Engineering

WHERE DID YOU PURCHASE THIS PRODUCT?

CUSTOMER NAME

mspress.microsoft.com

Microsoft Press, PO Box 97017, Redmond, WA 98073-9830

OWNER REGISTRATION CARD **Register Today!** 0-7356-0877-6

Return the bottom portion of this card to register today.

After the Gold Rush: Creating a True Profession of Software Engineering

FIRST NAME   MIDDLE INITIAL   LAST NAME

INSTITUTION OR COMPANY NAME

ADDRESS

CITY   STATE   ZIP

(   )

E-MAIL ADDRESS   PHONE NUMBER

U.S. and Canada addresses only. Fill in information above and mail postage-free.
Please mail only the bottom half of this page.

**For information about Microsoft Press®
products, visit our Web site at
mspress.microsoft.com**